When FOOTBALL *Was* FOOTBALL

LEICESTER CITY

First published in 2014

A catalogue record for this book is available from the British Library

ISBN: 978-0-85733-671-2

Published by Haynes Publishing, Sparkford, Yeovil,
Somerset BA22 7JJ, UK
Tel: 01963 442030 Fax: 01963 440001
Int. tel: +44 1963 442030 Int. fax: +44 1963 440001
E-mail: sales@haynes.co.uk
Website: www.haynes.co.uk

Haynes North America Inc., 861 Lawrence Drive,
Newbury Park, California 91320, USA

Images © Mirrorpix

Creative Director: Kevin Gardner
Designed for Haynes by BrainWave

Printed and bound in the US

When
FOOTBALL *Was*
FOOTBALL

LEICESTER CITY

A Nostalgic Look at a Century of the Club

Ralph Ellis

Contents

Filbert Street in the 1960s.

Foreword

A few months ago I was leaving the company of a few old friends in a south Nottinghamshire village. Dusk was setting in as I started the homeward journey. Something made me divert my tracks and head towards the old city of Leicester, in fact to Filbert Street, which had been my home for a while in the latter part of the last century.

    The stadium no longer exists, and to the unsuspecting eye it would be hard to imagine that the very piece of hallowed ground on which I was now standing had housed a wonderful football club for over a hundred years.

    One can still make out the main car park, and therein, despite new buildings now housing the students of Leicester's various educational institutions taking the place of the old 'Double Decker', history still abounds.

    Terraced thousands echoing in glorious unison. Their sound can still be heard above the students' conversation. For four and a half years I was part of that history. Yes, despite inauspicious beginnings to my tenure, it was an unforgettable period of my life.

    Darkness has descended but the noise seems to grow louder and louder. The roar of the crowd greeting victory coupled with the unquenchable strains of joy emanating from the dressing room.

    I think fondly of the team that was assembled. Terrific footballers, wonderful characters. They did the playing, they did the winning. They formed not only a strong bond with each other but also with the supporters, the lifeblood of the club. Great days indeed.

    Leicester City has found a lovely new abode and a new generation of supporters, but Filbert Street will always be my home, and to have shared it with some of the greatest names in football was indeed a great privilege.

    I hope you will enjoy seeing all the wonderful pictures in this book, which tell the stories of those who shared the club's adventure before us.

Martin O'Neill

Memorable moments for Martin O'Neill and Leicester's fans in one of many trips to Wembley.

Leicester Fosse
1884-1918

1884 Group of young churchgoers pay nine old pence each to buy a football – and a further nine old pence as subscriptions to form Leicester Fosse; first game played v Syston Fosse on 1st November on a field off the Fosse Road. 1885 Move to Victoria Park as home ground. 1886 Membership reaches 40 and a reserve team is founded. 1887 Move to Belgrave Road Sports Ground. 1888 Outbid by rugby union club in an attempt to buy Belgrave Road, and return to Victoria Park. 1889 New home in Mill Lane. 1890 Become full members of the Football Association. 1891 Entry to the Midland League; Filbert Street is opened as the new home ground. 1894 Entry to the Football League. 1898 Dick Jones and Ernie Watkins picked for Wales and become the club's first internationals.

It began with nine old pennies. That was how much each of the original group of players agreed to contribute to a fund to buy a football. Some of them were former pupils of Wyggeston Boys School, some were also linked to a bible class run in the old Emmanuel Church in New Parks Street. They met – according to legend – in a garden shed at the back of a house next to King Richards Road Chapel in the spring of 1884 and decided to form a football club under the name of Leicester Fosse that would begin playing games the following season.

Frank Gardner, elected that night as the first secretary and treasurer, suggested each should add a further ninepence as a subscription. And with those funds he set to work to engage a carpenter to build some goalposts in time for the first match to be played on 1st November that year.

They wore black jerseys with a diagonal blue sash and a team with an average age of 16 won their first fixture by five goals to nil against Syston Fosse.

An aerial view of Leicester City, 1926.

1900 Wooden terracing replaced by earthwork banking to create Spion Kop end. 1903 Kit changes to royal blue shirts with white shorts. 1904 Successfully apply for re-election after finishing bottom of Division Two. 1908 Goalkeeper Horace Bailey picked for England; promoted to First Division after finishing runners-up in Division Two. 1909 Relegated again. 1910 New signing Ted Pheasant tragically contracts peritonitis and dies two weeks after signing. 1912 Club announces a loss of £1,498 on the season. 1913 A summer trip to Sweden is the club's first foreign tour. 1915 Successfully applied for re-election after finishing 19th in Division Two; Football League programme suspended owing to the outbreak of the First World War.

Leicester City and the Daily Mirror

Football was seen as a secondary sport in Victorian England. Cricket, horse racing and rugby union held the public's attention. In Leicester in particular, rugby was considered the strongest winter sport. But as a new century began, the drama of football and its growing popularity began to create a change in status.

The *Daily Mirror* was launched at the end of 1903, and a few months later began to recognize the importance of recording Football League results. Leicester Fosse were first mentioned in February 1904.

The coverage of sport was a far cry from today's multi-page pull-outs and minute detail, but the paper recognized the growing fascination around an emerging competition which would have the power to both unite – and divide – the country.

This cartoon in September 1905 identified the change in the public's sporting obsession which was gathering momentum. The newspaper would go on charting the fortunes of the sport – and of Leicester City – until the present day.

SATURDAY'S RESULTS.

ASSOCIATION.
THE LEAGUE.—Division I.
Newcastle United (h), 0; Derby County, 0.
Sunderland, 3; Blackburn Rovers (h), 1.
Sheffield Wednesday, 1; Notts Forest (h), 0.
Aston Villa (h), 3; Stoke, 1.
Wolverhampton Wanderers (h), 1; Derby County, 1.
Bury (h), 2; West Bromwich Albion, 1.
Small Heath, 2; Liverpool (h), 0.
Middlesbrough (h), 3; Everton, 0.

Division II.
Manchester United (h), 1; Woolwich Arsenal, 0.
Leicester Fosse (h), 2; Bolton Wanderers, 2.
Preston North End, 1; Burslem Port Vale (h), 0.
Grimsby Town (h), 0; Burnley, 0.
Bristol City (h), 2; Barnsley, 0.
Blackpool (h), 0; Chesterfield, 0.
Burton United (h), 5; Lincoln City, 2.
Gainsborough Trinity (h), 2; Stockport County, 2.

SOUTHERN LEAGUE.—DIVISION I.
West Ham United (h), 4; Wellingborough, 1.
Tottenham Hotspur (h), 7; Reading, 4.
Southampton (h), 2; Fulham, nil.
Kettering (h), 2; Millwall, 1.
New Brompton (h), 2; Queen's Park Rangers, nil.
Luton (h), 1; Plymouth Argyle, 1.
Portsmouth, 1; Swindon (h), nil.
Northampton (h), 2; Brighton and Hove Albion, 2.
Bristol Rovers, 2; Brentford (h), 1.

DIVISION II.
Fulham R. (h), 4; Southampton R., 1.

FOOTBALL ELBOWS CRICKET OUT OF ITS WAY.

CRICKET: Now then, off-side! Don't be in such a hurry. Just remember I'm the national game.
FOOTBALL: Ah! you once were, Cricket, but I'm the national game now.
[The football season begins to-day.

11

–LEGENDS–

Horace Bailey

The son of an iron moulder from Derby, Horace Bailey was the man who began Leicester's tradition of providing top-quality goalkeepers. A good all-round sportsman who also played county standard tennis for Derbyshire, he began his working life as a railway clerk while playing in goal for Derby County reserves. He went on to appear for England's amateur team while also starring for the Great Britain side which won the gold medal in football in the 1908 Olympics. He joined Leicester Fosse in 1907 and made a significant contribution to the team which won promotion to Division One a year later.

Reports at the time said he had "an eye like a hawk, and a cat-like agility". He made his full England debut in a 7-1 win against Wales in Wrexham in 1908, and played four more times for his country that summer on a tour of Austria, Hungary and Bohemia. He returned to Derby after Leicester Fosse were relegated in 1909, playing for Blackburn, Stoke and Birmingham before enlisting in the Royal Engineers during the First World War.

> " *An eye like a hawk, and a cat-like agility.* "

ENGLAND BEAT WALES AT WREXHAM.

Game Spoilt by Accidents to the Welsh Players.

GRAND FORWARD DISPLAY.

At Wrexham yesterday Wales suffered a crushing reverse by seven goals to one, but the Principality were distinctly unlucky in losing the services of Roose and Hughes in the first half. England scored three goals with only nine men against them, and then, shortly after half-time, Dai Davies, the old Bolton goalkeeper, came out and deputised for Roose by permission of the English authorities.

It is impossible to judge the moral effect of the loss of Roose's services to the Welsh team, but England played such brilliant football that victory would have gone to the visitors in any event, and no one regretted the depletion of the Welsh team more than the Englishmen.

There was an eleventh-hour change on each side, H. P. Bailey, a Leicester Fosse amateur, keeping goal for England instead of Hardy (injured), and Matthews, of Caester, taking the place of L. Jones in the Welsh attack. It was a terribly depressing day, with bad light and some rain, but fortunately the snow had disappeared from the playing pitch, which was in fairly good order.

The game opened very fast, with two big efforts of Meredith saved by Bailey. Gradually the English forwards settled down, and after eighteen minutes' play Hilsdon bowled Roose over whilst the Welsh custodian was hugging the ball.

The goalkeeper got the worst of it, and had to retire, C. Morris going into goal. England immediately forced three corners, and from the last Woodward cleverly headed the first goal. Hughes soon after left the field through illness, and the game became too one-sided to be interesting. Grand footwork by Rutherford and Woodward enabled Windridge to score, and this was followed by Wedlock scoring from close quarters.

Wales were hopelessly outplayed, and after Morris had saved grandly from Rutherford, Hilsdon met the ball and scored easily. Meredith missed badly from a penalty-kick given against Crompton for charging Davies over, and England led by 4 to 0 at the interval.

In the second half Davies came out to keep goal, but Wales could make little progress, and only grand saving by the old Bolton custodian kept the score down. Eighteen minutes elapsed before Hilsdon headed through from Rutherford's centre. The sixth and seventh goals were grandly scored by Woodward from Hilsdon's passes, and then in the last minute Wales were awarded a free-kick just outside the penalty line, from which Davies shot into the net.

The English team played very fine football. Pennington at left-back was particularly safe; the halves were brilliant, and Lintott's shadowing of Meredith made the Welsh captain lose his temper badly.

The forward play was absolutely fascinating, and Woodward never gave a more superb display, despite the attentions of Parry, who was by no means particular in his methods. The English captain shot three goals, and all were gems of the first water. Hardman was a distinct improvement on Wall at outside left, and Rutherford, Windridge, and Hilsdon all played well, their close footwork completely bewildering the Welsh defence.

Morris and Blew defended pluckily for Wales, and Latham worked hard at centre half. The forwards were held in check by the English halves throughout.

ALFRED DAVIS.

LEFT: Wales 1, England 7. The *Daily Mirror*'s report of Horace Bailey's England debut.

FOOTBALL –STATS–

Horace Bailey

Name: Horace Peter Bailey

Born: July 1881

Died: August 1960

Playing career: 1899–1912

Clubs: Derby County, Crich, Ripley Athletic, Leicester Imperial, Leicester Fosse, Derby County, Blackburn, Stoke, Birmingham

Leicester appearances: 68

England appearances: 5

A Brief – But Sour – Taste of the Big Time

Fosse spent most of the early part of the 20th Century struggling to deal with a series of financial difficulties as the directors fought to find a way to produce a competitive team while balancing the books. But in the 1907–08 season things came together in spectacular fashion.

Optimism began with work to extend both the main stand at Filbert Street and the Spion Kop, which expanded the capacity to 22,000.

The side lost only one of its first 11 matches, and was further strengthened by signing centre-forward Fred Shinton from West Bromwich Albion at the start of December. From the turn of the year they lost only at Fulham, and even survived the decision to sell 19-goal top scorer Percy Humphreys to Chelsea.

Sadly the new status did not last. Shinton was injured for most of the early part of the next campaign, and a dreadful run from early October to the start of March brought only one victory. His return helped spark a brief run of hope, including a win away to FA Cup finalists Manchester United. But other results that day had already confirmed Fosse would be relegated – and four days later came the shock of a 12-0 hammering away to neighbours Nottingham Forest which was the subject of a League inquiry (although Leicester were cleared of any wrongdoing).

PROMOTION FOR LEICESTER.

The Fosse, After Years of Striving, a First League Club.

By a victory over Stoke, at Stoke, yesterday, by a goal to nil, Leicester Fosse, for the first time in the history of the club, are promoted to the First Division.

That the success that they have attained is well deserved it is almost needless to add, for during recent years they have season after season finished high up in the Second Division table, and last year were next to the promoted clubs. One year they were beaten by goal average only.

The final placings of the first three clubs are:—

	P.	W.	L.	D.	Goals For	Agst.	Pts.
Bradford City	38	24	8	6	90	42	54
Leicester Fosse	38	21	7	10	72	47	52
Oldham Athletic	38	22	10	6	76	42	50

Had Leicester been beaten Oldham would have gone up on goal average.

Leicester's win yesterday was quite a meritorious one, and when Shanks scored twenty-five minutes from the start the result never seemed in doubt, although after the interval Stoke made great efforts to equalise.

Great satisfaction was felt in Leicester last night when it became known the Fosse had its effect, for, although some of their earlier performances were disappointing, they have put up some great struggles since Christmas, and never gave up striving for promotion even when their chance seemed hopeless.

The obvious improvement of the Fosse in the last two years has already had its effect, and this season Association football in the town has obtained many converts, and on several occasions the Fosse have had gates of 20,000—a number undreamt of three years ago.

The Fosse's record for the season includes the least number of lost games in either division. Queen's Park Rangers, in the Southern League, have lost one less, but they have still two matches to play.

	Plyd.	Won.	Lost.	Drwn.	Goals For	Agst.	Pts.
Manchester City	36	15	17	4	66	66	34
Aston Villa	36	12	14	10	53	55	34
Liverpool	37	14	17	6	56	65	34
Bury	37	13	16	8	59	75	34
Chelsea	35	12	14	9	52	57	33
Nottingham Forest	36	12	16	8	50	56	32
Bradford City	35	10	16	9	41	45	29
Leicester Fosse	35	8	18	9	52	85	25

It is interesting to note that both next Saturday's finalists at the Crystal Palace were beaten, Manchester United by Leicester Fosse, the bottom club of all, and Bristol by Sunderland. The last-named scored a wonderful victory at the Western seaport by 4 to 2, after Bristol had led by a couple of goals at the interval. Sheffield Wednesday were too good for Everton, and ran the rule over them by 2 to 0.

Of the other matches in the Second League the best performance was accomplished by Hull City, who outplayed Fulham at Craven Cottage and beat them by 3 to 0, a score which does not exaggerate their superiority. The thrustful, speedy, and heavy Hull forwards were always quite on top of the Fulham defence, which was made to look slow and hesitating. Clapton Orient were beaten at Oldham, and the Blackpool and Chesterfield clubs, who are struggling to get out of the last three places, were, like Stockport, on the losing side.

In the Scottish Cup final on the Hampden Park ground at Glasgow the Rangers and Celtic played another draw, and the crowd rioted because they would not continue the struggle to the bitter end. A full account of the trouble will be found on page 5.

Clapton won the Amateur Cup comfortably from Eston United, and, after a disgraceful game, in which one of the players of the Metrogas side was ordered off the field, Dulwich Hamlet carried off the Surrey Senior Cup.

There are several good games in town to-day. At Tottenham England meets Belgium in the amateur international. The final of the London F.A. Professional Cup between Leyton and Millwall will be played at Upton Park, and Northampton, the prospective champions of the Southern League, will be on show at Park Royal in a Southern League match with the Rangers.

CITIZEN.

GOAL AVERAGE.

Notts Forest Improve Theirs by Scoring 12 to 0 Against Leicester.

Notts Forest, evidently thinking that goal average may count in the question of which clubs are to fill the last two places in the League table, went all out for a big win yesterday, and beat Leicester Fosse by 12 goals to 0. It was cricketing weather, and the players evidently made up their minds to give Nottingham sportsmen a foretaste of the summer pastime.

Leicester were not at full strength, Aitken and Durrant being unable to play, and Pollitt and Holding taking their places. On the other hand, Notts had the veteran Morris back in their side. There were 6,000 spectators, and the display of the Forest aroused them to a great pitch of enthusiasm.

Playing against the wind, the Forest made a phenomenal start, scoring four goals within ten minutes. The first came from Morris. Then Spouncer got through twice in succession, and Hooper shot the fourth. Spouncer scored a fifth goal from a penalty kick, given against Gorman. West registered the sixth point, Hooper the seventh, and Hughes the eighth. At half-time the Forest led by 8 goals to nothing.

Iremonger, the Forest goalkeeper, was only once seriously tested in the first half, and then by a rattling shot from Donnelly. The Fosse forwards had been completely outclassed, save for West and Donnelly. They displayed little better form in the second half.

Five minutes from the resumption Morris scored a ninth goal for the Forest, who continued to press in irresistible manner. West brought the total into double figures, and also shot the eleventh goal. Hooper brought up the round dozen with a splendid shot.

This gives the Forest a better goal average than any of the sides still in the danger zone, but would they have done it if the Fosse had had a chance of keeping in the First League? In the words of Harry Tate, Joe Elvin, and Co., "Yes, I don't think."

The clubs in danger are now:—

	P.	W.	L.	D.	Goals For	Agst.	Pts.
Notts County	37	14	16	7	49	46	35
Manchester City	36	15	17	4	66	66	34
Aston Villa	36	12	14	10	53	55	34
Liverpool	37	14	17	6	56	65	34
Bury	37	13	16	8	59	75	34
Nottingham Forest	37	13	16	8	62	56	34
Chelsea	36	12	15	9	52	60	33
Bradford City	36	11	16	9	44	45	31
Leicester Fosse	36	8	19	9	52	97	25

Phoenix from the Flames
1919-1939

John Duncan leads out Leicester's team before an FA Cup replay at Filbert Street against Hull in February 1925. Arthur Chandler scored a hat-trick (one of 17 in all during his career for the club) in a 3-1 win. Sadly City were knocked out by Cardiff in the next round, but went on to win promotion to the First Division that season.

1919 Change of name to Leicester City Football Club and the club becomes a limited company; Peter Hodge appointed as first secretary-manager with full control of team. **1921** New main stand built at Filbert Street. **1923** Inside-forward Arthur Chandler signed. **1925** Promoted as Second Division champions. **1926** Peter Hodge resigns to become manager of Manchester City, and is replaced by Willie Orr. **1927** New 'Double Decker' stand built at Filbert Street. **1928** Ground record 47,298 in attendance to see FA Cup tie v Tottenham. **1929** Runners-up to Sheffield Wednesday in Division One. **1930** Captain John Duncan quits football after Leicester sack him for taking over the licence of a public house. **1932** Willie Orr resigns as manager; Peter Hodge returns. **1934** FA Cup semi-final v Portsmouth; Peter Hodge dies suddenly in Scotland; Arthur Lochhead becomes new manager. **1935** Adam Black plays the last of a club record 528 games; City are relegated after finishing 21st. **1936** Arthur Lochhead resigns after two games of the new season, replaced by Frank Womack; club record £7,500 fee brings Jack Bowers from Derby. **1937** Promoted as Second Division champions after 4-1 win over Tottenham on 1st May. **1939** City finish bottom; new season suspended owing to the outbreak of the Second World War.

When Fosse Became City

The First World War focused minds on problems far greater than the poor performances of the 1914–15 season which had caused Leicester Fosse to apply for re-election to the Football League after finishing 19th of the 20 clubs.

Former reserve player Lt Col Bernard Vann, who was awarded the Victoria Cross for charging a field gun at the front of his men, was among those with connections to Fosse who failed to return from the battlefields of France. Many other ex-players were seriously injured.

By 1919, as peace returned, it was clear that the club which had continued playing in the wartime Midland League was now close to going out of business, with debts to the Midland Bank of more than £3,000.

An extraordinary meeting led by chairman WH Squires was held to discuss winding up the club, and forming a new company to take it over. The resolution was passed – as it happened a few days after a royal visit by King George V had paved the way for the town of Leicester to be reinstated as a city after some 700 years.

Some £10,000 was raised in shares to float the new company, and so it was decided to mark the start of the new era by leaving behind the name 'Fosse' and begin the 1919–20 season in August under the name of Leicester City Football Club.

ABOVE: The result of the first game under the title of Leicester City is recorded.

BELOW: A report of City's second game under their new title – a defeat at Tottenham.

GREAT RUSH TO LEAGUE MATCHES.

Half a Million People Present at Thirty-Three Games —Unparalleled Enthusiasm.

LEFT & ABOVE: The *Daily Mirror* records the excitement of the resumption of League football.

SPURS' SECOND WIN.

Enthusiasm at Tottenham Over Success of North London Side.

(TOTTENHAM, 4; LEICESTER, 0.)

Never has greater enthusiasm been shown at a season's opening at Tottenham. There must have been 30,000 people present and the cheering was practically continuous throughout the game, which was won by the 'Spurs by 4 to 0.

Leicester City played really fine football and did not deserve to be beaten pointless. Still, the 'Spurs should have scored more goals than they did.

In the first minute the Tottenham goal had a narrow escape, when Norton nearly barged Jacques through his goal with the ball in his hands. Then Macaulay missed a sitter, and Jacques had to save a stinging shot from Douglas.

After that the Tottenham forwards got going and many shots were fired at the Leicester goal without greatly troubling Boon. After a quarter of an hour Currie, the Leicester left back, ballooned the ball in front of his own goal and Cantrell headed it through. This was the only goal of the first half, although the 'Spurs attacked hotly up to the interval.

Leicester had all the best of the opening stages of the second half, but could not beat Clay at right back and Jacques in goal. Twice the goalkeeper saved well from Douglas when an equaliser looked like coming.

Then the 'Spurs got going and the forwards found a splendid game. First Walden, by brilliant dribbling, made an opening for Cantrell to score. Then Cantrell was tripped when right through and Clay scored from the penalty kick. To make matters sure Chipperfield made a beautiful opening for Bliss to score the fourth goal. Leicester were unlucky not to score, but were well beaten.   M.

There were nine directors on the new City board, and even though at first they raised barely a quarter of the £10,000 working capital they wanted, there was still much optimism about a new start.

Their promise was to strengthen the team, develop Filbert Street, and to renegotiate the lease on the ground from the City Corporation to put the club into a strong position to move forwards.

But one other decision could be argued to have had the biggest effect on achieving their aims – the appointment of Peter Hodge as secretary-manager.

Hodge, who had experience of running clubs having held similar positions at both Raith Rovers and Stoke, was handed full responsibility for team matters in what was – for the time – a bold step into a new age. Many other clubs at the time were still relying on their committee or board of directors to pick the team each week.

Hodge, then a 50-year-old, had begun his football career as a referee and moved from there to administration, but possessed a shrewd eye for a player and an astute tactical brain.

He was to build his team around two key signings – captain John Duncan, who followed him from Raith, and centre-forward Arthur Chandler. It took time, but by 1925 City were storming into the top flight as Second Division champions.

–LEGENDS–

John Duncan

An imposing, creative right-half or inside-forward, Duncan was born in Fife in Scotland and first played football for Lochgelly United in the wartime Eastern League. It was there that he was spotted by Peter Hodge and recruited for Raith Rovers – and when Hodge moved to Filbert Street he was the player the new secretary-manager most wanted to follow him south. It took three years of persistence to make the move happen, and only then because Leicester also signed his brother Tom. But the wait was worth it, as Duncan became the key man around which Leicester's promotion campaign was built.

As captain he insisted the club stay loyal to the passing style even when Hodge left to become Manchester City manager. Under his leadership Leicester not only achieved promotion, but were a force in the First Division, finishing third in 1928 and then runners-up – missing out behind Sheffield Wednesday by just one point – a year later.

FOOTBALL –STATS–

John Duncan

Name: John Duncan

Born: February 1896

Died: March 1966

Playing career: 1915–30

Clubs: Lochgelly United, Raith Rovers, Leicester City

Leicester appearances: 295

Goals: 95

Scotland appearances: 1

A Promotion Season

Hodge had been building a team steadily after taking over, and in the summer of 1924 signed full-back Harry Hooper from Southampton and winger Harold Wadsworth from Liverpool. He also promoted Duncan, who had already proved his leadership qualities on the field, to be the club's captain.

The campaign didn't start so well with a 1-0 defeat at Manchester United on the opening day, but two days later Hodge's side gave notice of their potential with a 4-0 win at home to Chelsea.

But it was from the start of December that they really hit their stride, losing just one of their remaining 25 fixtures.

By the end of the campaign Duncan had scored 30 goals, while Chandler's three hat-tricks included scoring five in a 6-0 thrashing of Barnsley.

They wrapped up the Second Division Championship title on the final day and celebrated at Filbert Street in style – even if the London editions of the newspapers might have been ready to move on to summer sports!

GLOOMY PENSIONERS.

Chelsea Lose at Leicester, but Palace Win at Coventry.

Chelsea attracted 25,000 people to the Filbert-street ground when they met Leicester City. The Londoners were outplayed, and only great work by Howard Baker kept the score down.

Chandler was entrusted with a penalty kick in the first half, but this Baker stopped. Adcock was the only man to beat him in the first half, a fine oblique drive leaving him helpless. Chandler scored the second after the breather, and Carr added the other two. The discomfiture of Chelsea was complete.

Scoring three times in the last twenty minutes, Crystal Palace gained a great victory over Coventry in the Midlands by 4 goals to 1. Coventry attacked hotly at the beginning, but the Palace defence was great.

Hamilton scored the first goal for the Londoners, but Pynegar equalised from a penalty. Whitworth and Blakemore subsequently found the net, the last named twice defeating the goalkeeper.

The meeting of the Wednesday and Derby County produced a grand game, which the County won, Storer scoring the only goal in the last half-minute. The Wednesday were a shade the better side, but Olney repeatedly saved Derby.

GOOD-BYE. FOOTBALL

Huddersfield, Leicester, Swansea and Darlington Champions.

SEASON WHICH IS TOO LONG

Football is dead for the season. It lived a week too long, really. It is a far cry from the last Saturday in August to the first in May, and everyone seems glad when the curtain is rung down.

The League champions are Huddersfield in the First Division, Leicester City in the Second and Swansea and Darlington respectively in the Third Divisions South and North.

With the exception of Darlington, the issue had been in doubt almost up to the last. Leicester were safe for promotion, and the championship some days ago, and so were Darlington, but until the last kick yesterday promotion from the Third Southern was in doubt.

Another goal by Exeter against Swansea and Plymouth would have gone up on goal average.

It is bad luck to be pipped on the post, by a short head, but I think Swansea were a trifle more consistent as a team than the Argyle.

West Bromwich were going to carry off Cup and League, we were told, but with two goals before them, failed in both, so that Huddersfield, last year's winners, retained the title.

Derby County, in the Second Division, for a long time looked and played like champions. In the end they did not even secure promotion, Leicester City and Manchester United passing them in the home straight.

–LEGENDS–

Hugh Adcock and Ernie Hine

John Duncan's leadership and Arthur Chandler's goals made them the brightest stars of Leicester's new First Division team, but Hodge's skill as a manager was to make sure there was a creative spark in the side to provide the ammunition for the goalscorers.

He found winger Hugh Adcock playing locally for Loughborough, and nurtured his talent in the reserves before bringing him into the team at the same time as signing Chandler.

Inside-forward Hine's £3,000 transfer fee from Barnsley was an indication of the ambition that City were showing after moving into the top flight.

Hugh Adcock (left) and Ernie Hine having a knockabout in training.

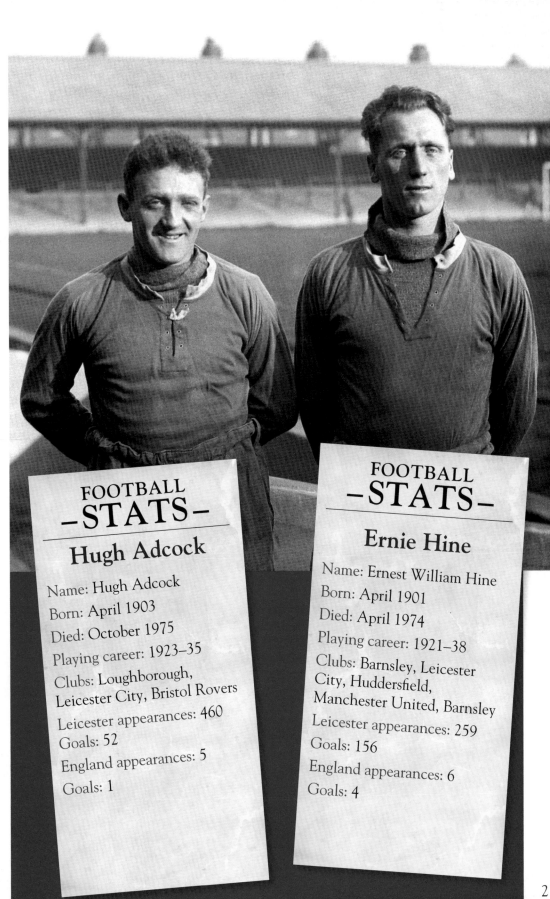

FOOTBALL –STATS–

Hugh Adcock

Name: Hugh Adcock

Born: April 1903

Died: October 1975

Playing career: 1923–35

Clubs: Loughborough, Leicester City, Bristol Rovers

Leicester appearances: 460

Goals: 52

England appearances: 5

Goals: 1

FOOTBALL –STATS–

Ernie Hine

Name: Ernest William Hine

Born: April 1901

Died: April 1974

Playing career: 1921–38

Clubs: Barnsley, Leicester City, Huddersfield, Manchester United, Barnsley

Leicester appearances: 259

Goals: 156

England appearances: 6

Goals: 4

–LEGENDS–

Arthur Chandler

Peter Hodge had a gift for finding players who he thought could improve – and never showed that better than in the signing of Arthur Chandler.

The London-born centre-forward had worked on a bookstall at Paddington station and then as a gardener after returning from duty in the First World War, and had played amateur football before joining Queens Park Rangers.

At the age of 27 he had scored just 16 goals in three seasons at Loftus Road, and his move to Filbert Street in the summer of 1923 was expected to be mostly to provide reserve cover.

Instead Chandler proved himself a strong and courageous leader of the line, and he went on to set scoring records which may never be broken.

The club's all-time record scorer with 273 goals, he also hit the most hat-tricks (17), the most in a single season (34 twice), and the joint highest in a single game (six in a 10-0 win against Portsmouth in 1928).

A man of great humour and also considerable tactical nous, he is also the club's oldest scorer, getting his final goal at the age of 39 years and 34 days.

GOSSIP ON THE LEAGUE GAMES
Chandler's Five Goals Against the Villa—Gallacher Surprises the Spurs—Sunderland's Victory

OLD-TIMERS gasped when they read that Chandler, of Leicester City, had routed Aston Villa by scoring five goals against the mighty Brums. Chandler was never appreciated at Shepherd's Bush, and was transferred by Queen's Park Rangers to Leicester, and since then has become one of the stars of the First League firmament. Badly as the Villa were hit, we shall see them coming out before long, and without the aid of players bought from other clubs for many thousands of pounds. Tradition counts, and new blood will come along at Aston.

TALE OF SIX SWANS

I have heard of players dreaming what would happen in Cup-ties, etc., but the story about Arthur Chandler's goal-scoring feat for Leicester on Saturday beats them all.

When Chandler had scored his fifth goal against Portsmouth, five swans flew over the ground. Then another swan flew after the first batch, and Chandler promptly scored a sixth goal. Leicester ought to secure the transfer of these swans.

A. Chandler.

TR/, TRY AGAIN

Stanton, Oldham's centre-forward, was responsible for his team's second win of the season, and on his performance should keep his place in the first eleven. It was from Taylor's corner kick that Stanton breasted the ball past the Chelsea custodian, after many previous disappointing attempts.

Stanton only made seven appearances last season, and netted three times.

FOOTBALL
–STATS–

Arthur Chandler

Name: Arthur Clarence Hillier Chandler

Born: November 1895

Died: June 1984

Playing career: 1920–35

Clubs: Queens Park Rangers, Leicester City, Notts County

Leicester appearances: 419

Goals: 273

CHANDLER'S REVELS

Arthur Chandler, Leicester City's London-born centre-forward, had a day out. He notched four of Leicester's five goals scored on Newcastle's ground. Hine got the other goal for the City. It was a black day for the Geordies, whose old hands could not get going. Their solitary goal was scored by Chalmers, who was making his debut in Newcastle's ranks.

City in Training

Paul Moss and goalkeeper James McLaren training. Tragically Moss, who scored five times in 18 reserve games, was just 19 when he collapsed in a practice match and died days later of meningitis.

A year after gaining promotion, Peter Hodge suddenly left to take charge of Manchester City, and Willie Orr was handed the manager's role.

Under his guidance, City grew as a force in the First Division, only to twice miss out on the title.

They finished third in the 1927–28 season, winning only two of their final six matches to stumble at the final hurdle, and then a year later were runners-up just an agonizing point behind League champions Sheffield Wednesday and with a better goal difference.

RIGHT: George Ritchie, who took over the captaincy when John Duncan left.

–LEGENDS–

Adam Black

City's all-time Football League appearance record holder proved his courage long before he became a fearless right-back at Filbert Street – he won the Distinguished Conduct Medal during the First World War as a corporal in the Argyll and Sutherland Highlanders.

Discovered in Scotland by Peter Hodge, he spent 16 seasons as the rock of Leicester's defence, ever present in four of them and missing just one game in three more.

The only mystery was why the Scottish selectors considered him too small and slight to pick for his country – in every other aspect but physical appearance he was a giant of a man.

FOOTBALL –STATS–

Adam Black

Name: Adam Black
Born: February 1898
Died: August 1981
Playing career: 1919–35
Clubs: Bathgate, Leicester City
Leicester appearances: 557
Goals: 4

RIGHT: Reg Osborne and Adam Black try skipping to keep fit.

All the club's progress was undone in one incident. John Duncan had wanted to secure his future for the end of his playing days by taking over the licence of a nearby pub.

However the roots of Leicester's creation from a Methodist chapel meant this was specifically forbidden, and the board voted to sack arguably their greatest player.

All of a sudden a club which had spent a few seasons competing at the top end of the First Division was in the middle of the table and then fighting to stay up.

Orr resigned in January 1932 after a run of six defeats, but even the return of Peter Hodge couldn't halt the slide.

Hodge narrowly won three relegation fights before his tragic and sudden death in the summer of 1934 – but an 8-0 defeat at Arsenal that December, shown in these pictures, signalled just how far Leicester had fallen.

By the end of that season they were back in Division Two. Former Birmingham defender Frank Womack briefly enjoyed success by winning promotion in his first year in charge in 1937, but could sustain the new status only until 1939. By the time the Second World War broke out, Leicester were not only back in the Second Division once more, but Womack was among officials being investigated by the FA over accusations of irregular payments.

John Duncan in the manager's chair at Filbert Street.

Postwar FA Cup Adventures
1940-1949

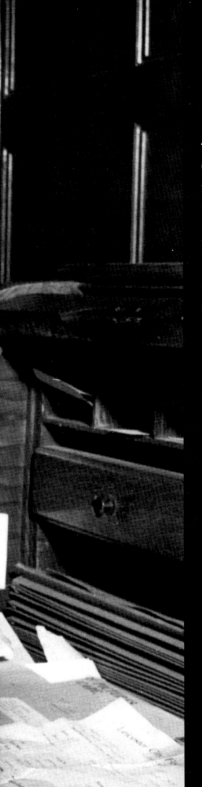

A Legend Returns

City were 90 minutes from a first Wembley appearance but lost to Arsenal in the semi-final of the Football League War Cup in 1941, but otherwise there was little to take minds away from the greater problems of the hostilities in Europe.

Relegation just before the outbreak of war took a toll off the field – especially when an FA inquiry began looking into the club's books.

They were looking for evidence of excessive bonuses and signing-on fees as well as irregular payments to amateurs. A two-day inquiry ultimately saw five directors suspended from football for life, and former manager Frank Womack banned for a year and fined £500.

Four other directors got shorter bans, while in total 12 current and former players also ended up with year-long suspensions.

There had even been talk during 1940 of putting the club into liquidation, but the formation of a supporters' club, with 1920s captain John Duncan on its committee, encouraged the newly constructed board to fight for the club's survival.

Maybe that was why, as peace was returning to Europe and Tom Mather resigned his post in charge of team affairs, the club gave Duncan – whose spell as a player had ended in such acrimony – the chance to build a new future.

"

He has insisted the way to success was by expert use of the ball.

1940 Leicester are censured by the FA and fined £500 for making irregular payments to players. Former manager Frank Womack fined £500 and suspended for 12 months. Five directors suspended *sine die*. **1941** Main stand at Filbert Street suffers substantial bomb damage. **1942** Fire causes further extensive damage to the stadium. **1944** Wartime manager Tom Bromilow resigns to be replaced by former Stoke and Newcastle manager Tom Mather. **1945** Mather himself moves on and John Duncan is invited back to the club to take charge. **1946** Filbert Street lease extended after local council agree by just one vote. **1948** Club crest worn on jerseys for the first time; deal to sign Peter McKennan from West Brom in exchange for Jack Haines and cash is valued at a club record £10,600. **1949** FA Cup final v Wolves (lost 1-3); John Duncan asked to resign, Norman Bullock appointed manager with a "five-year plan".

A Return to Traditions

Back in the 1920s it had been Duncan who, as skipper, did most to develop the Leicester way of playing, with passing and control.

After being given the chance to manage the club, he was determined to return to those old standards and recruited players of technical quality.

The first season of a return to League football in 1946 began with more than 28,000 packed into Filbert Street, and a run to the FA Cup fifth round raised spirits even further.

These 1947 pictures, with the main stand being rebuilt in the background, were taken as Duncan's side prepared for a replay against Newcastle.

LEFT: Defender Sep Smith was a key figure in the postwar teams.

RIGHT: George Dewis, who scored 62 goals in 81 wartime matches.

Goalkeeper Joe Calvert.

–LEGENDS–

Mal Griffiths

The *Daily Mirror* forecast a bright future for 18-year-old Welsh prospect Mal Griffiths when he made his debut for Arsenal against Leicester.

Little did the writer – or anybody else – know that the youngster's career would end up reaching legendary status not at Highbury but at Filbert Street.

Griffiths had too many top players in front of him at Arsenal, and agreed to a £750 transfer move north later that year.

The Second World War interrupted Griffiths' career – he was the first City player to be conscripted and joined the Welsh Regiment. But one of John Duncan's first moves on taking charge was to send director Leslie Green across the border to Wales to convince Griffiths to return to playing football for a living.

It proved an inspired move. The tricky right-winger starred for City for another 12 seasons, playing 409 games as well as winning 11 caps for his country.

He scored seven of his 76 for the club in the run to the 1949 FA Cup final – including City's solitary goal in the final.

FOOTBALL
–STATS–

Mal Griffiths

Name: William Maldwyn Griffiths

Born: March 1919

Died: April 1969

Playing career: 1935–57

Clubs: Arsenal, Leicester City, Burton Albion

Leicester appearances: 409

Goals: 76

Wales appearances: 11

Goals: 2

ALL JOIN IN TO SHARE ARSENAL RUNAWAY VICTORY

Arsenal 3, Leicester City 1

ARSENAL were not flattered by their win over Leicester City. Londoners were faster more polished and had high-power shooting forwards.

Griffiths, making his League debut, played craftily. There is a big future predicted for this eighteen-year-old right winger.

Drake shot the only goal of the first half, Bastin the second, after the change over, and Jones got Arsenal's third.

Leicester's goal came from a penalty taken by Smith.

Male, Hapgood and B. Joy were inviolate in the Arsenal defence, and Leicester were so overplayed at times that the home full backs took part in attacks.

Once Hapgood dashed the length of the field, beating man after man, before finishing with a terrific shot which struck the side netting.

Drake played a vigorous game, and Bastin was always dangerous. Hunt and Jones were not at their best.

Griffiths.

SAINTS SHATTER DEFENCE

Southampton 2, Bradford 1

Better side throughout the match at The Dell deservedly won.

Farr saved splendidly from Holt and Bates in the first half, when Osman struck a post with a terrific effort, but a quarter of an hour after the interval Osman put Southampton in front.

Bevis soon added, but Lewis immediately responded for Bradford. Osman again hit an upright.

Wembley Here We Come!

Excited fans arrive in London for Leicester City's first ever appearance in an FA Cup final.

John Duncan's brief was to build a side that could restore Leicester to the First Division, but despite two ninth-place finishes in 1947 and 1948, his team played good football but couldn't find the consistency they needed to reach the top of the Second Division table.

The next season was even worse in the bread and butter of the Football League – but little of that mattered as Duncan's side went on a run in the FA Cup.

It didn't start so well – they needed two replays to get past Birmingham City in the third round. But with another of Duncan's signings Don Revie – later to find fame as manager of Leeds and England – pulling the strings from inside-right they played some superb football to see off Portsmouth in the semi-final at Highbury.

It was a huge shock. Pompey were First Division leaders at the time and eventually won the Championship.

Leicester's reward was the first outing to an FA Cup final in their history.

Big cheer for new Cup giants —by five boys

By JOHN THOMPSON

WIDE-EYED and excited, holding autograph books and pencils, five small boys raised a cheer outside the deserted Leicester City ground as the new favourites for the F.A. Cup arrived yesterday for treatment for injuries.

The applause of the little group which had waited patiently for a glimpse of their idols was a piping echo of the roar which had thundered across Arsenal Stadium as Leicester players were mobbed by supporters after their 3—1 conquest of Portsmouth.

Perhaps there was a lesson for those boys in the manner in which City have found unbelievable triumph at last. The leaders of the League were beaten by men who had nothing to lose save pride in their own craftsmanship.

Many despised their chances and scoffed at their confidence. Yet even through the jeering of their own followers, unfancied, struggling against relegation, they held fast to the idea of playing football as it should be played—with culture and imagination.

That was how they played at Highbury. The ball was swung sweetly into open spaces, tackling was sharp and clean.

Fine Teamwork

It was one of the finest displays of teamwork and understanding I have seen for a long time. Portsmouth need not be ashamed of their defeat.

Leicester trainer George Ritchie spoke for the others when he said: " It's a strange feeling—to think we'll really be at Wembley."

One player pointed out that they were now 6—4 favourites—cause for reflection by men who once saw themselves listed as 400—1.

Manager Duncan's instructions at half-time were based on a judgment made soon after the start.

" I saw Portsmouth's left flank could be pierced and told the lads to concentrate on playing down the right to Griffiths." he said.

Both wingers, Adam and Griffiths, former Arsenal player were outstanding. They received perfect support from Revie, who scored twice, and Chisholm Leicester's other scorer. The ball went in off Scott for Portsmouth's goal.

ABOVE: FA Cup training. Ken Chisholm (left) and Mal Griffiths take part in a dribbling race while the other players look on.

RIGHT: FA Cup skipper Norman Plummer in training at Filbert Street.

LEFT: How the *Daily Mirror* reported the semi-final.

–LEGENDS–

Don Revie

History casts Revie as the manager of the Leeds side that dominated football in the 1960s, then sadly failed to transmit that success to England.

But Revie's association with Leicester brings better memories. Signed as a teenager, he emerged as a skilful playmaker under the guidance of John Duncan, recovering from a broken ankle to play a key role in the 1949 FA Cup run.

In fact his impact was so strong that Leicester appealed to the FA for him to be given a special runners-up medal after he'd missed Wembley because of burst blood vessels in his nose.

He left Filbert Street not long afterwards to join Hull in a £20,000 move, then made his way via Manchester City and Sunderland to Elland Road.

FOOTBALL –STATS–

Don Revie

Name: Donald George Revie

Born: July 1927

Died: May 1989

Playing career: 1944–62

Clubs: Leicester City, Hull, Manchester City, Sunderland, Leeds United

Leicester appearances: 110
Goals: 29

England appearances: 6
Goals: 4

A Close-Knit Team

LEFT: Leicester's FA Cup finalists try on their kit and meet their mascot.

BELOW: *The Walls of Jericho* – starring Hollywood glamour actress Linda Darnell – was the entertainment of choice at Stevenage Cinema two nights before the final.

LEFT: A team meal after training at Filbert Street.

Life for a footballer in the 1940s was a far cry from today's world of fast cars and fashion – even for a player on his way to the FA Cup final.

These pictures were taken of full-back Ted Jelly, who joined the club after being demobbed from the Navy and broke into the side on New Year's Day 1949.

He took over from the injured Willie Frame, and stayed in the side all the way to Wembley.

"Nice of Your Wife to Wear Blue, Sir"

Despite their giant-killing act over Portsmouth in the semi-final, Leicester were massive underdogs against First Division Wolves. And their problems grew deeper when Don Revie, the 21-year-old whose two goals in the semi-final at Highbury had earned their trip to Wembley, suffered a nosebleed three days before the final. It left him too weak to leave hospital to watch the game, never mind play.

Manager Duncan did his best to ease the nerves. Princess Elizabeth was guest of honour, together with the Duke of Edinburgh, attending an FA Cup final for the first time. When Duncan saw the future Queen of England had chosen an outfit that matched City's colours, he famously tried to get the royal consort on his side.

Manager John Duncan prepares to shake hands with the Duke of Edinburgh before the FA Cup final. Charlie Adam (next to Duncan) and Ken Chisholm look on.

A Grand Day Out

It's Odds On The Wolves

BUT ANYTHING CAN HAPPEN IN THE CUP—AND AT WEMBLEY

By JOHN THOMPSON

WRAP up "the old tin pot" and give it to Billy Wright. Tell the silversmiths to engrave the name of Wolverhampton Wanderers against the Cup Final of 1948-9. No need for speculation, no need to wait till the cheers have faded and the game is over.

I know that's the way you feel this morning. It's the opinion of every Soccer follower I have met. Leicester are given so little chance that it seems almost a waste of time for them to go to Wembley at all.

Common sense, form, the merits and records of the two teams, both in defence and attack, all point to a walkaway win for Wolves. A First Division manager who has studied them both wanted to bet me last night that Wolves would win—and he was willing to give Leicester three goals start.

His view that Wolves' brilliant wingers would rip through Leicester's doubtful defence was a reasonable argument.

NOT REMEMBER THE CUP'S MAGIC LAUGHS AT REASON AND MAKES NONSENSE OF FAIR JUDGMENT

Remember, too, the power of City's resilient spirit. Knocked reeling by injuries and relegation fears, without Don Revie their greatest player, they have an accountably remained one of the most cheerful Final sides I have ever visited.

Think for a moment of the pomp and tension of this afternoon—and these luckless Second Division players joking over their superstitions and mascots in their dressing-room before they go out.

CAN EVEN WOLVES BEAT THE LEICESTER SPIRIT? I THINK NOT. I TAKE LEICESTER TO WIN. AFTER SEEING THEM LICK PORTSMOUTH I BELIEVE THE IMPOSSIBLE IS PROBABLE.

Manager John Duncan is confident. "We will win."

Rag ball in an alley was the start of his success

PICTURE on alley 101, wide and a boy there, kicking a ball made from old socks and tied together with string.

Then picture him sitting wide-eyed while a Soccer-loving restaurateur explains the craft and tactics of the game by moving twenty-two painted corks across a board marked as a football pitch.

HOW THEY'LL LINE UP

WOLVERHAMPTON WANDERERS

Williams

Pritchard   Springthorpe

Crook (W.)   Shorthouse   Wright

Hancocks   Smyth   Pye   Dunn   Mullen

Referee: R. A. MORTIMER, Huddersfield

Adam   Chisholm   Harrison (J.)   Lee   Griffiths

King   Plummer   Harrison (W.)

Scott   Jelly

Bradley

LEICESTER CITY

THE RIVAL CAPTAINS

The 'Clincher' can do it again

THEY call Malvyn Griffiths the "Clincher." Leicester City's outside right (above) has the art of putting finishing touches to movements. A match-winner.

The men of Oakengates are still very shy

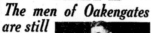

IN the streets of the Shropshire market town of Oakengates a boy rolls on a football.

HOW THEY GOT THERE

ON the way to Wembley, Leicester have scored twenty-one goals in eight games and conceded fifteen.

KEY BATTLES IN LEAGUE

PROMOTION and relegation problems may be the issue...

ABOVE: How the *Daily Mirror* saw the game on the morning of the FA Cup final.

RIGHT: Leicester's fans wait for the action to begin at Wembley.

41

A Story of What Might Have Been

Wolves, with the great Billy Wright marshalling their defence, lived up to their status and dominated the first half to take a two-goal lead into the interval. Yorkshireman Jesse Pye scored both of them. But five minutes after the interval came the moment Leicester fans were hoping for, as Ken Chisholm's shot was only parried by Wolves goalkeeper Bert Williams and Mal Griffiths followed up to score (main picture).

That gave the Second Division side new hope, but luck was not on their side, despite Princess Elizabeth's choice of outfit.

Chisholm ran on to a Griffiths pass to score from close range, only to turn away and find the linesman's flag ruling him offside – despite claims the ball had touched a defender on the way to him which under the rules in those days meant the goal should have stood.

It was a critical moment – minutes later Irish winger Sammy Smyth set off on a 40-yard dribble that took him past three Leicester defenders before slotting the ball out of the reach of goalkeeper Gordon Bradley.

Leicester's season hadn't ended at Wembley – they still had three vital Second Division matches remaining to ward off the threat of relegation.

Duncan was determined that they should see their achievement of reaching the final as a victory, and the *Daily Mirror* of the time reflects how well he got that message home.

Instead of returning directly to the East Midlands, the manager took the team away to Brighton for some seaside air.

When they got back to football, they realized his plan had worked – a 2-1 win over Bury was followed by a draw at Cardiff which secured their safety by a point and sent Nottingham Forest into the Third Division instead.

BELOW: Autograph hunters follow Leicester's FA Cup final players on the front at Brighton the day after the match.

Eleven men of Leicester find glory in defeat

By JOHN THOMPSON

THERE was a time when I went to visit a bruised and beaten boxer. Along the corridor the new champion was surrounded by admirers. They slapped his back and drank to his victory. The man he had battered was alone and an old fighter looked in and said to me quietly: "There's no place so lonely as a loser's dressing-room. He's forgotten by them all."

I know now it is not true always. I know because I saw eleven Second Division footballers from Leicester waiting on the field below the royal box at Wembley.

Wolverhampton Wanderers went laughing up the steps to take the F.A. Cup.

They stood there not knowing what to do with themselves, and some of them tried to grin. A few clapped self-consciously. Then their own time came and they went up to receive the medals given to losers.

And suddenly there was a roar from the crowd. I didn't expect it. There might, I thought, be a murmur of sympathy. But this was a great swelling cheer. It was very English. Very moving. It was sincere acknowledgment that victory can be found in defeat. Glory in failure.

How splendidly Leicester had earned the applause! Beaten 3—1, with Don Revie their greatest player, in hospital, disorganised and often outplayed by powerful and confident opponents, they had rallied and fought back.

Two goals down at half-time, their chances looked hopeless to everyone except themselves. In the dressing-room John Duncan, their manager, advised forward changes and told them: "You can win this game yet."

In the room next door Stanley Cullis talked to his happy men in black and old gold. All he said was: "Keep playing the kind of football you have been playing."

Within two minutes Duncan's switch gave Leicester a goal. "Clincher" Harvey Griffiths finishing a movement made by Ken Chisholm.

Leicester attacked. We rubbed our eyes.

Wild with Delight

Supporters went wild with delight as Chisholm rushed forward and rammed the ball into the net. The Bury Boys jumped up and waving his arms rushed back towards the centre.

But the referee had ruled him offside.

Let Chisholm himself tell you about this saddest of all the Cup's "if only" stories.

"I ran into position and Jim Harrison kicked from the wing. I thought he would put it...

Instead he tapped to Mal Griffiths and Mal hooked it to me. I saw the goalkeeper was beaten and banged it. I must have gone crazy for a moment.

"The thought of being offside never entered my head. I was sure it was a goal, and dashed twenty yards up the pitch before I realised it had been disallowed.

"I believed we were level, and that we could go on and win.

"If only it had been that way—I'd have gone on running till I was shaking hands with our supporters on the terraces. You'd have needed a hose to catch me."

Referee R. A. Mortimer had no doubts. He told me: The decision was my own and I only knew later that linesmand had signalled simultaneously. I saw the whistle before Chisholm kicked the ball. He was definitely offside.

Leicester had not recovered from their disappointment when Sam Smyth added to the two goals scored by Jesse Pye.

The Final 'Whoof'

"Leicester players were pulling away, expecting me to pass so I went on by myself." Then I 'whoofed' it as hard as I could.

The Irishman's "whoof" put the finishing touch to Wolves' fine win.

Apart from Wright's masterly play I give credit to their winners, John Hancocks and Jim Mullen. Leicester failed because there was no connecting link between half backs and forwards.

It was in the distribution of the ball that Wolves most showed their superiority.

Leicester backs and halves tackled with determination, but too often nervously wasted their passes. They swung into their normal, smooth rhythm only in the first ten minutes of the second half.

Had Don Revie been playing there would have been fewer gaps. His skill and judgment would have steadied the whole team.

Duncan summed up: Every Wolverhampton goal was caused by our side trying to clear too hurriedly.

At their party after the returned from Wembley they told me how they had sent a telegram to Revie — promising him they would bring home the Cup.

They could still join Norman Plummer, their young captain, said: "Now we'll have to send another saying: 'Apologies—the new atmosphere, unforeseen circumstances.'"

Revie, think, must be very proud this morning to know how hard his friends tried to keep their promise to him. The result of a game of football is still less important than the spirit in which it is played.

THE THRILL OF A LIFETIME

AMONG the 100,000 Cup Final spectators were two men in hospital blue.

They were Bill Parker, 49, of West Hendon, Middlesex, and Bill Butler, 20, of Bideford, Devon, patients at Queen Mary's Hospital, Roehampton.

Neither had seen a Cup Final before. "It's been a thrill of a lifetime," they said after the match.

As no reader gave the correct forecast in our competition to name the two Cup Final clubs, the donor of the tickets decided to give the two tickets to wounded ex-Servicemen.

BOOMER DIES

Mr Percy Boomer, 64, professional to the Sunningdale Golf Club since 1920, has died at his home.

A KISS FOR THE VICTOR

Billy Wright and his team-mates took the Cup home in triumph yesterday, and one of the first to welcome him was his landlady, Mrs Annie Colley.

"It was the happiest moment of the happiest day of my life," said the Wolves captain after the match.

It is as certain as anything can be in sport, writes John Thompson, that without Wright Wolves would have lost. His leadership was inspiring, and in both defence and attack he did the work of three men.

Mrs Annie Colley kisses her lodger, Billy Wright, as he holds the Cup.

The toast of the town

RAICH CARTER is the toast of Hull. In his first full season as player-manager, he has put the club back in the Second Division after sixteen years.

Now his big job will be to strengthen his side and prevent Hull falling back in a season to the Third Division as Doncaster and Lincoln have done.

"But we have tough times ahead," Raich said after Saturday's game against Stockport, which made Division III (N) championship certain.

Of Hull's six goals Raich scored two, centre forward Moore three, and Jensen one. Alex Herd got Stockport.

Victory Dance

To mark their promotion the club's directors will hold a dinner on Wednesday, after the last home League match, against Doncaster.

For a victory dance next week, the supporters' Club, 7,500 strong, have booked the City Hall. The club's vice-chairman and presidents are staging a celebration dinner.

BIGGEST FIGHT IS P

IT'S going to be a tight finish in the race to avoid relegation to the Second Division.

Only three points separate the last four clubs—Middlesbrough, Sheffield United, Preston and Huddersfield.

Remaining fixtures are: Middlesbrough away to Manchester United and Aston Villa; Sheffield United, away to Manchester United, and home to Newcastle United and away to Wolves and Liverpool; Huddersfield home to Wolves and Manchester City.

Preston, with two hard matches, both away from home, are in a desperate plight.

Manager Will Scott last week took the players to Blackpool in the hope that the new atmosphere would do good.

They returned there after surrendering a point to Bolton at Deepdale, and are in good heart for the remaining games.

They were fortunate to draw with Bolton.

They panicked when Bolton equalised and with each man trying to score the...

LAST-LAP FIGHTS

DIVISION I

	Goals
	F. W. D. L. F.A. Pts
Middlesbro	40 11 11 18 46 35 33
Shef. U.	40 12 10 18 50 70 33
Preston	40 10 11 19 50 58 31
Huddersf'ld	40 10 10 20 35 59 30

DIVISION II

	Goals
	F. W. D. L. F.A. Pts
Notts F.	41 15 7 21 49 54 33
Leicester	39 9 16 15 58 74 32
Lincoln	41 7 12 22 50 81 31

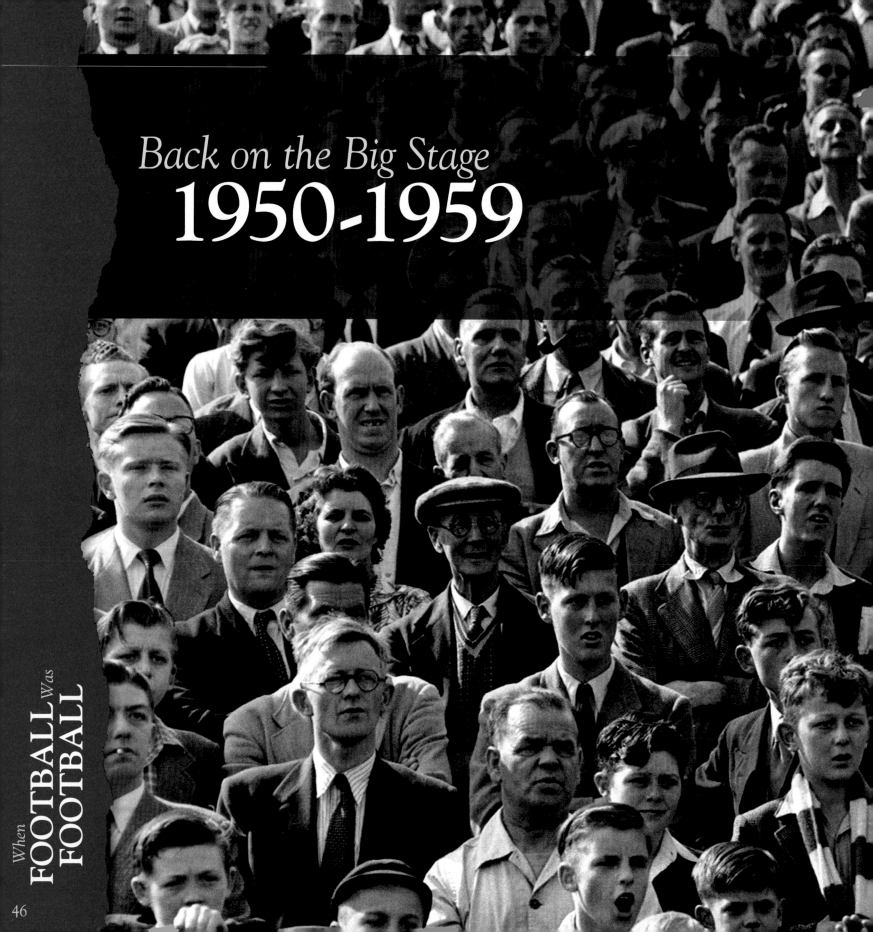

Back on the Big Stage
1950-1959

Hats, scarves, pipes, tension. A snapshot of the Filbert Street crowd watching a game in 1957.

1950 New manager
Norman Bullock signs
Arthur Rowley from
Fulham for £14,000.
1951 Maximum wage for
players raised to £14 per
week. **1953** Rowley sets
new club record of 41 goals
in a season. **1954** Leicester
promoted back to Division
One as champions. **1955**
Bullock asked to resign after
an incident at a Whitley
Bay hotel in February;
chairman Len Shipman
takes over the team who
get relegated; David
Halliday appointed as new
manager. **1957** Division
Two champions; floodlights
installed at Filbert Street.
1958 Arthur Rowley
allowed to leave after
265 goals in 321 games;
David Halliday resigns,
coach Matt Gillies is new
manager. **1959** Gordon
Banks joins the club.

Leicester City in action in an away game at Fulham in 1952.

The Five-Year Plan

If John Duncan's first spell at the club as captain had ended acrimoniously, then there was just as much bitterness surrounding his departure from the manager's role.

Bigger clubs were casting envious eyes on the players who had taken Second Division City to the FA Cup final, and there were rumours that several wanted to take the opportunity to move on.

Don Revie was appointed captain for the new season, but by September had submitted a transfer request which was granted. Duncan didn't want to sell, and held out for a part-exchange deal of some sort, but the directors wanted to cash in on a player who had emerged as their prime asset.

By October, with the club struggling through a run of four defeats in a row, Duncan was asked to resign and did so – before making it very clear he felt he had been sacked.

The directors took over the task of picking the team, but when results failed to improve they turned to Norman Bullock to be the new manager, with instructions to produce a five-year strategy that would lift City back into the First Division.

As an ex-centre-forward, holder of Bury's appearance record as well as three England caps, he knew a good goalscorer when he saw one and his plan began with the purchase of Arthur Rowley for just £14,000 from Fulham.

Leicester fans saw it as a cheap way to replace the popular Jack Lee who had been sold to Derby for £2,000 more. When Rowley scored on his debut on the first day of the 1950–51 season it was an encouraging sign – but only the beginning of the goals that were to follow.

MANAGER 'SACKED'

J. DUNCAN.

MR. JOHNNY DUNCAN, former player, and manager of Leicester City since 1946, resigned his appointment with the club yesterday at the request of the directors.

Mr. L. T. Shipman, chairman, stated: "Mr. Duncan was asked to go by the board. There is no personal friction between us, and I hope there never will be."

Mr. Duncan said: "All I can say is that I am no longer manager of the club. I have simply been sacked."

Mr. Duncan last season took the club to the Cup Final for the first time in their history. He went to Leicester City from Raith Rovers in July, 1922, and played with them until 1930. He was top scorer at Leicester in his first season, the best the club had experienced in fifteen years.

FIRST DIVISION

Aston Villa 2, W.B.A. 0; Burnley 0, Arsenal 1; Charlton 4, Bolton 3; Chelsea 4, Sheffield W. 0; Everton 3, Huddersfield 2; Manchester U. 1, Fulham 0; Portsmouth 1, Middlesbrough 1; Stoke 1, Newcastle 2; Sunderland 1, Derby 0; Tottenham 1, Blackpool 4; Wolves 2, Liverpool 0.

SECOND DIVISION

Barnsley 1, Southampton 2; Bury 2, Leicester 3; Grimsby 0, Cardiff 0; Leeds 3, Doncaster 1; Luton 2, Brentford 0; Notts C. 0, Coventry 2; Preston 3, Manchester C. 4; Q.P.R. 1, Chesterfield 1; Sheffield U. 0, Blackburn 3; Swansea 0, Birmingham 1; West Ham 3, Hull 3.

THIRD DIVISION (S.)

Bournemouth 1, Bristol C. 0;

WELL—WHAT MORE COULD A SUPPORTER WANT FOR HIS 1s. 9d.?

By BOB FERRIER

LEICESTER beat Fulham 6—1 last night, and, believe me, everything happened — all the incident and drama and madness that only football in all the entertainment world can provide.

There was Arthur Rowley, Leicester inside left, against his former club, playing with a little extra zest in his game, and power in the boots, hammering four merciless goals past Fulham.

There was the penalty-kick, first of these four, always a sure teller with the crowd.

There was Ian Black, Fulham goalkeeper, injured, off, back on, the scorer of a great but solitary Fulham goal, and indeed their best forward.

There was Bobby Brennan, Fulham's best forward until then, moved into goal, and providing a gallantly lighthearted interpretation of the art of keeping it safe.

Could thirty thousand people ask for anything more—at 1s. 9d.? It seems there is always something happening at Leicester.

Rowley started it, after a few minutes, with a thunderous penalty goal then, as his centre forward Hines cleverly ducked and Black dithered, headed another, from the right half Baldy Baldwin. Time — 17 minutes.

Then Black injured his elbow, went off. Bobby Brennan, who had done the few clever Fulham frontal things at inside left, went into goal, a strange decision. Time 30m.

So pleased was he that he scampered beyond the penalty area carrying the ball. The Fulham defence thought it was a "non-scoring" kick. Arthur Rowley didn't. He smashed the ball straight in. Time 40m.

Black came back into the attack wearing the Fulham white shirt and, from centre-forward, headed a superb goal from a Stevens cross, in the manner of Dixie Dean. Time 46 mins.

But it was too good to be true, for a football writer, that the transplanted goalkeeper could save the side from the centre-forward position, and Rowley, Hines and Griffiths showed little sympathy for Fulham's misfortunes, making it the round half-dozen

Leicester? A strong, determined, hard-working side. They will be threatening furiously this season.

Fulham? With heavy heart, I must say of them "This is where we came in."

RESULTS

DIVISION I

Blackpool .. 1 Preston 1
Marston o.g. Wayman
Wolves .... 3 Bolton 1
Swinbourne 2, Moir
Broadbent

DIVISION II

Hull ...... 1 West Ham .. 0
Gerrie
Leicester .... 6 Fulham 1
Rowley 4, Black
Worthington
Griffiths
Sheffield U. . 1 Everton 0
Brook

DIVISION III (S.)

Q.P.R. ..... 2 Watford 2
Gallogly o.g. Thompson 2
Smith

DIVISION III (N.)

Barrow ..... 1 Stockport .. 0
Gordon
Bradford .... 2 Rochdale ... 1
Horsman, Whitworth
Turner
Halifax .... 3 Hartlepools . 2
Priestley 2, McGuigan,
Frost Willetts
Mansfield ... 2 Gateshead .. 0
Reeve, Coombe
Port Vale .. 2 Tranmere .. 0
Mullard,
Griffiths
Southport .. 2 Workington . 0
Hitchin,
Musgrave
Wrexham ... 2 Bradford C. 1
Tunnicliffe, Dix
Hewitt

...centre-forward, they weren't ...only two more goals in the six matches that followed his debut.

That was when Norman Bullock shifted him to the number 10 role behind Derek Hines, and the man who became known as 'The Gunner' started firing at full force.

Three goals at home to Bury on 16th December brought the first of 16 hat-tricks for the club and he ended his first season with 28 goals.

A year later it was 38, then 41 in 1953 to break Arthur Chandler's club record and set a standard which is unlikely ever to be beaten.

His 33 in 1954 included vital efforts in a run to the FA Cup quarter-finals, and more importantly shot City to the Second Division Championship as Bullock's team achieved his plan of a place in the First Division a year ahead of schedule.

Rowley got in another 23 in the First Division, even though Leicester's promotion lasted only a season – so Rowley simply hit 44 goals in an ever-present campaign to put them back to the top once more.

After moving on to Shrewsbury, his eventual haul of 433 goals from 619 League games remains a Football League record.

FANS' LONG WAIT WAS WELL WORTH WHILE

By BILL HOLDEN

Leicester C. 4, Blackburn R. 0

FOR three and a half hours before kick-off time fans queued to get into the ground for this vital promotion battle. And they found it well worth the wait.

They cheered with aban-don every time Leicester even lobbed the ball into the Blackburn half, and had thrills galore in the first session.

The thrills began early, and in the twenty-third minute Leicester went ahead.

Arthur Rowley placed the ball for Hines, and when the centre forward's shot was blocked, Rowley himself blazed the ball in with a grand shot.

Mal Griffiths appealed in vain for a goal when his shot hit the Blackburn crossbar, and seemed to re-bound down over the line and then come out again.

A minute before the interval, Johnny Morris increased Leicester's lead when he ran in and hit a perfect right-foot drive out of the reach of Reg Elvy.

No. 3

Within six minutes of the restart, Morris in-creased Leicester's lead. This time a Rowley shot was blocked and it was Morris who was on hand to slash it into the net.

Eddie Russell played out a magnificent second half with a huge white bandage around his forehead cover-ing a bad face cut.

There were near-misses galore before Arthur Row-ley crashed in Leicester's fourth goal four minutes from the end. And there it is, the promotion problem is still wide open.

Leicester hit back— into First Division

By GEORGE HARLEY

BRENTFORD went down to the Third Division fighting valiantly but vainly to deny Leicester the points which meant promotion to the First. Yet they did Leicester two big favours— by scoring for them and against them.

First, left back Ken Horne put through his own goal to give the Midland-ers a half-time lead they did not deserve. Leicester seemed content to protect this advantage even if meant figuring in Soccer quizzes as " the team that gained promotion by win-ning a match without scor-ing."

Fine Pass

Then, twenty minutes from the end, Dudley equalised from a fine pass from Bloomfield. A ripple of anguish ran through the 10,000 Leicester fans pre-sent.

Their team rose superbly to the emergency and, within a minute, Griffiths restored the lead. Four minutes later he surprised the Brentford defence with a quick throw-in and the unmarked Morris gave Leicester a 3—1 victory.

And there, I think, lies the reason for Leicester's success this season, and the promise of a bright First Division future. They have spirit, resilience and deter-mination to back the skill and scoring power that have produced a club re-cord of ninety-seven League goals.

Brentford's ill-luck pur-sued them to their last game. Two first - half efforts by Billy Dare merited goals.

And that own goal . . . listen to Ken Horne, back in the team for the first time since Boxing Day: "It's the first time I have ever put the ball through my own goal. Small's shot from the left hit the post and the ball struck me on the thigh and went in before I could get out of the way."

–LEGENDS–

Tom McArthur

The star performers attract the headlines and the glory – as well as the places in history – at every football club.

But football is a team game and just as vital are the men who loyally provide the back-up and cover for injuries.

McArthur, a tall and tough former Scots Guardsman, is included in Leicester's roll call of legends to represent all those who gave commitment and determination to the cause without ever getting any of the glamour.

He spent eight seasons at Filbert Street, and was a regular at centre-half in only one of them, but his contribution as captain of the reserve side and as an understudy to Sep Smith, Norman Plummer and Matt Gillies, made him a vital part of the fabric of the club.

FOOTBALL –STATS–

Tom McArthur

Name: Thomas McArthur

Born: April 1925

Died: April 1994

Playing career: 1946–53

Clubs: Leicester City, Plymouth Argyle

Leicester appearances: 97

A Fair Day's Pay

Leicester's troubles with the FA over excessive payments to players in the 1930s made their directors conscious of the need to follow the rules to the letter, as austerity continued to bite in Britain in the 1950s.

In 1951, after a campaign by the players, the Football League agreed to increase the maximum wage payable to professionals by £2 to £14 per week.

At a time when the average working man in a factory or office earned around £10.50, it was a good rate of pay – but hardly enough for a luxury life. Nowadays it would be the equivalent of earning around £600 a week.

Clubs like Leicester ran strong reserve teams as well as their first team, so competition for places was always intense.

Even a star performer like Welsh International Mal Griffiths, pictured here practising his dribbling skills at Filbert Street, had to make sure he stayed at the top of his game to earn his pay rise.

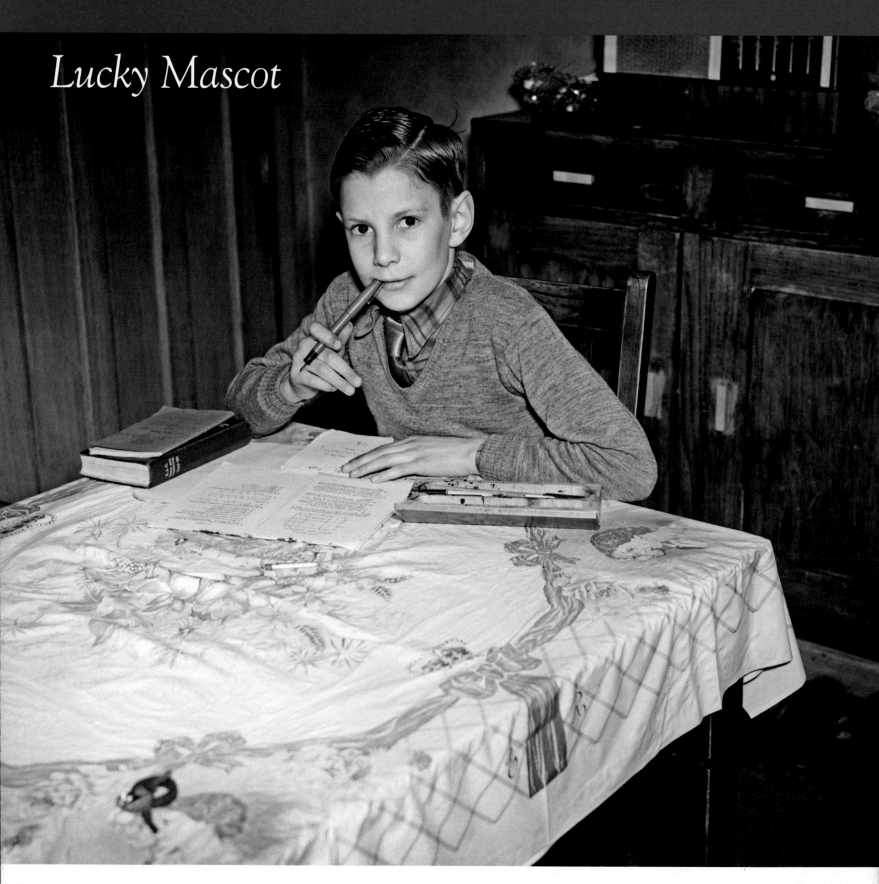

Lucky Mascot

Football in the 1950s was a far cry from today's commercial world, but there were the beginnings of clubs attempting to develop their image.

Leicester's staff recruited this young lad as the club's official mascot in 1954, and his influence inspired a run to the FA Cup quarter-final, eventually losing to Preston only after two replays in front of a crowd of 44,356 at Hillsborough.

Match Action

Bullock's team started the 1953–54 campaign well, but fell away in the middle of the winter and there were fears that yet another attempt at promotion might end in disappointment.

After leading the table from mid-October, by the end of January they had dropped to fifth place after losing 3-1 at Nottingham Forest. But then came Rowley to the rescue, as his goals sparked a run of five wins in a row including a 4-1 demolition of Swansea at Filbert Street shown in these pictures.

Mud, Sweat and Tears

Today's players are used to pitches that have every blade of grass finely manicured. 1950s football was a very different matter, as these pictures of Leicester's 1956 FA Cup tie at Luton show all too clearly.

City won the game 4-0 thanks to yet another Arthur Rowley hat-trick, but lost to Stoke in the fourth round after a replay.

OUT! SOCCER'S BIGGEST SPENDER

★
Storer may get the job

STORER   BULLOCK

By BILL HOLDEN

NORMAN BULLOCK, Leicester City manager, who took the club back to the First Division last season, resigned yesterday for "personal and private reasons."

He had been with the club six years. In that time Leicester have spent £200,000 in transfer fees—more than any other club.

Mr. Bullock's successor will probably be Harry Storer, former Birmingham and Coventry manager.

Expected to Return

Mr. Storer was expected to return to Soccer management soon with a Midlands club, and he is likely to be offered the Leicester job.

Mr. Bullock, a former England centre forward, was manager of Chesterfield and Bury before moving to Leicester six years ago.

He built up the team that won promotion last season. The club is now last but one in the table and in serious danger

Neither Mr. Bullock nor the Leicester directors would amplify a joint statement in which the Board said the resignation had been accepted with regret.

Last big signing by Mr. Bullock was the £30,000 transfer of Andy Graver from Lincoln in December

Second Shock

Leicester directors had a second shock for their supporters yesterday when they announced that Johnny Morris, former England international inside right, had been suspended for fourteen days from last Monday for an alleged breach of discipline.

Mr. Charles Maley, Leicester secretary, told me:

"Mr. Bullock's resignation and the suspension of Morris are in no way connected."

Morris said last night: "I expected the suspension but I cannot comment on it. It is not a serious matter and there is no question of my asking for a transfer.

"Mr. Bullock's resignation does surprise me. It is not connected with my suspension at all."

First Division Failings

Norman Bullock's five-year plan was designed to put City into the top flight, but having spent more than £160,000 in assembling the side which won promotion, he failed to strengthen it sufficiently to deal with a First Division campaign.

By November he realized something needed to be done, paying £4,750 for defender Willie Cunningham, and a month after that smashed the club's transfer record again to buy centre-forward Andy Graver from Lincoln for £27,600.

It was too late to make much of a difference. Worse was that there were problems developing behind the scenes where Bullock had fallen out with a number of his players.

He had already been told his contract would not be renewed at the end of the season, when matters came to a head following an incident at a Whitley Bay hotel where the team were staying before playing Newcastle.

A board meeting the following day ruled that "it is impossible for the manager to conduct the affairs of the club or be able to control the playing staff". By the end of the week he had resigned.

City's directors took over the task of picking the team while ignoring applications for the vacant manager's post – and the relegation that followed was a sorry end to a year that had begun with so much optimism.

Return to the First Division

When Leicester's directors finally got round to looking for a new manager, they headed to Scotland to recruit David Halliday, who had been a centre-forward for Queen of the South, St Mirren and Dundee before moving south to score 153 League goals for Sunderland.

After a brief spell as player-manager for non-League Yeovil, he started his full-time managerial career at Aberdeen and went on to build the club before winning the Scottish title in 1955, a success which attracted Leicester's attention.

Though Bullock had spent big in the transfer market, Halliday concentrated on getting the best from the players he had inherited.

He produced a far more stable environment and got his reward when, with Arthur Rowley having the season of his life, his team stormed to the Second Division Championship.

They finished some seven points ahead of second-placed Nottingham Forest, confirming their promotion with a 5-3 win over West Ham four games before the end of the season.

PAGE 20   DAILY MIRROR, Monday, April 8, 1957

Mirror SPORT UP! LEICESTER HATS OFF TO ROWLEY

ARTHUR ROWLEY
Record buster

Spoiler Spurs shared spoils

By DEREK WALLIS
Man. Utd. 0, Spurs 0

SPURS spoiling tactics tamed the champions at Old Trafford.

Their plan was clear. All-conquering United's slick-moving attack must be blunted. They must not be allowed to score.

It was a negative plan ... a spoiling game. But so very effective.

Key figure in this tight defensive curtain thrown around the penalty area was Maurice Norman.

Normally a left back, he played a poised no-nonsense game at centre half.

Norman smothered England centre forward Tommy Taylor's precision work on the ground and in the air.

He followed him out to the wings and destroyed Taylor's link with the rest of the attack.

Even the wingers, Terry Medwin and Terry Dyson, figured in the defensive strategy.

They patrolled deep beats on the touch-lines, often throwing themselves into tackles against United's wingers.

TWO RECORDS BROKEN

Brentford 1, Colchester 1

ONE minute from time, Brentford captain Jeff Taylor soared to get a momentous 1—1 equaliser against Colchester.

It was a goal and point which could well keep top-of-the-table Colchester in the Third Division.

It was also a goal which set up two post-war records for Brentford, who have now gone sixteen successive home League matches without defeat, and also gone nine consecutive matches unbeaten.

Some said that Taylor was off-side when he scored. But Colchester player-manager Benny Fenton said: "It was a good goal."

For Colchester were lucky to survive a second-half hammering. And Fenton, who popped up as the extra reinforcement wherever danger threatened, was the man of the match, and scored his side's goal.

Leicester 5, West Ham 3

THE chief Soccer citizens of Leicester were quietly celebrating their return to the First Division with tea, whisky and pork pie in the board room after this triumph.

Then someone turned on the radio and they heard this summing-up of the England v. Scotland international:

"Both sides will have to get some goal-scoring for-

By Ron Beagley

wards for their World Cup Games..."

Almost everyone in the room turned to their neighbour and asked: "What about our Arthur for England?" Our Arthur being, of course, Rowley, their ace scorer and record buster.

This extract from my notebook will tell you why those happy people think that inside left Rowley should be given another chance to show his wares in representative Soccer.

● 3.9 p.m.: Rowley scores from McNeill's pass.
● 3.16: Rowley head in Derek Hogg's cross for his forty-second goal of the season—the most he has scored. This brought Leices-

ter's total for the season to 98—the most they have scored.

● 3.23: It's Rowley again for his hat-trick.
● 3.43: Rowley shakes his head in disbelief as goalkeeper Ernie Gregory saves one of his specials.

Rowley again tormented the West Ham defence in the second half. If his pals had not tailed off, he would have got more goals.

Outside right Billy Wright bagged Leicester's other two goals in the twenty-seventh and seventy-seventh minutes to take them over the 100 mark.

Malcolm Musgrove (twenty-four and seventy-eight minutes) and Malcolm Allison (eighty minutes), from the penalty spot, scored for West Ham.

DOWN We go fighting says Trotter

W.B.A. 2, Charlton 2

CHARLTON manager Jimmy Trotter sighed after watching his team drop a valuable point because of a penalty four minutes from time.

"It looks as if we're doomed," he said.

"But so long as we go down into the Second Division fighting, I shan't mind so much."

Charlton looked certain to beat a near-reserve West Bromwich team.

First Johnnie Summers, their tearaway centre forward, whipped in a pass from Stuart Leary in the thirty-first minute. Then outside right Sam Lawrie scored a minute after half-time.

But within fifty seconds Maurice Setters headed a brilliant goal, and then Jago gave away that penalty.

Fine—when they forgot Final

Chelsea 1, Aston Villa 1

FOR five dreadful minutes Villa threatened to commit Soccer suicide, writes Ross Hall. Thinking only of their Cup Final date, they held back in every tackle.

But after Peter Brabrook had put Chelsea ahead—in the fifth minute—Villa put the Final out of their minds. They equalised in the sixtieth minute through Jackie Sewell.

Chelsea worked tremendously hard. Their only trouble was lack of experience.

RON TAKES A POUNDING

Cardiff 0, Luton 0

CARDIFF would have had two points to ease their relegation worries—but for the superb goalkeeping and courage of Ron Baynham.

Luton's former England international was knocked out twice. His nose was cut and his front teeth loosened as he robbed battling Cardiff of the goals they deserved.

Football crowds were traditionally male-dominated, but in the 1950s Leicester City tried to encourage more women to attend.

It was part of attempts to modernize the club as they returned to the First Division.

This picture, taken in the first few months of the 1957–58 campaign, suggests that they had some success.

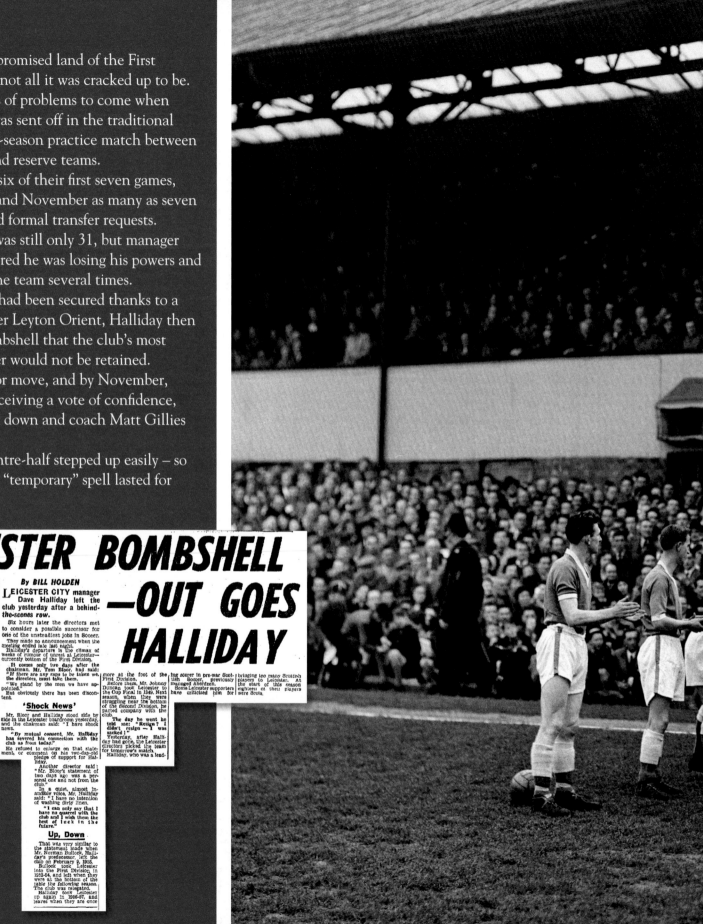

Once again the promised land of the First Division proved not all it was cracked up to be. There were signs of problems to come when Johnny Morris was sent off in the traditional Blues v Reds pre-season practice match between the club's first and reserve teams.

City then lost six of their first seven games, and in October and November as many as seven players submitted formal transfer requests. Arthur Rowley was still only 31, but manager Halliday considered he was losing his powers and left him out of the team several times.

Once survival had been secured thanks to a final-day win over Leyton Orient, Halliday then dropped the bombshell that the club's most prolific goalscorer would not be retained.

It proved a poor move, and by November, two days after receiving a vote of confidence, Halliday stepped down and coach Matt Gillies took charge.

The former centre-half stepped up easily – so much so that his "temporary" spell lasted for 10 years!

LEICESTER BOMBSHELL —OUT GOES HALLIDAY

By BILL HOLDEN

LEICESTER CITY manager Dave Halliday left the club yesterday after a behind-the-scenes row.

Six hours later the directors met to consider a possible successor for one of the unsteadiest jobs in Soccer.

They made no announcement when the meeting ended late last night.

Halliday's departure is the climax of weeks of rumour of unrest at Leicester—currently bottom of the First Division.

It comes only two days after the chairman, Mr. Tom Bloor, had said: "If there are any raps to be taken up, the directors, must take them.

"We stand by the men we have appointed.

But obviously there has been discontent.

'Shock News'

Mr. Bloor and Halliday stood side by side in the Leicester boardroom yesterday, and the chairman said: "I have shock news.

"By mutual consent, Mr. Halliday has severed his connection with the club as from today."

He refused to enlarge on that statement, or comment on his two-day-old pledge of support for Halliday.

Another director said: "Mr. Bloor's statement of two days ago was a personal one and not from the club."

In a quiet, almost inaudible voice, Mr. Halliday said: "I have no intention of washing dirty linen.

"I can only say that I have no quarrel with the club and I wish them the best of luck in the future."

Up, Down

That was very similar to the statement made when Mr. Norman Bullock, Halliday's predecessor, left the club on February 2, 1955.

Bullock took Leicester into the First Division in 1953-54, and left when they were at the bottom of the table the following season. The club was relegated.

Halliday took Leicester up again in 1956-57, and leaves when they are at once more at the foot of the First Division.

Before them, Mr. Johnny Duncan took Leicester to the Cup Final in 1949. Next season, when they were struggling near the bottom of the Second Division, he parted company with the club.

The day he went he told me: "Resign? I didn't resign — I was sacked!"

Yesterday, after Halliday had gone, the Leicester directors picked the team for tomorrow's match.

Halliday, who was a leading scorer in pre-war Scottish Soccer, previously managed Aberdeen.

Some Leicester supporters have criticised him for bringing too many Scottish players to Leicester. At the start of this season eighteen of their players were Scots.

HALLIDAY—" I wish them the best of luck."

The decade ended with Leicester still holding on to their First Division status, after a 2-0 win over Manchester United kept them above Portsmouth and Aston Villa.

Three days earlier they had been reminded just how much they still had to achieve in the top flight when they played at Molineux where Wolves had already been crowned champions.

Leicester's players formed a guard of honour to applaud Billy Wright and his team-mates onto the pitch.

PLAYERS AND OFFICIALS ONLY

The Swinging Sixties
1960-1969

Shake, rattle and roll – Leicester's young fans get in the spirit of the Sixties.

1960 Minimum admission price raised to three shillings. 1961 Reach FA Cup final losing to Spurs' double-winning side; Leicester go into European Cup Winners' Cup and play Atlético Madrid. 1962 Club purchase the freehold of Filbert Street. 1963 FA Cup final v Manchester United; finished fourth in Division One. 1964 League Cup final victory v Stoke; home match v Nottingham Forest is the club's first appearance on *Match of the Day*. 1965 League Cup final defeat to Chelsea. 1966 Peter Shilton makes his debut aged 16. 1967 World Cup-winning goalkeeper Gordon Banks is sold to Stoke. 1968 Leicester break British record to sign Allan Clarke for £150,000 from Fulham; manager Matt Gillies resigns in protest at having his assistant and coach sacked; Frank O'Farrell appointed as his replacement. 1969 FA Cup final v Manchester City and David Nish becomes the youngest FA Cup final captain; Leicester are relegated; Clarke is sold to Leeds for £165,000.

The Gentleman of Filbert Street

If it came as a surprise to many outside of Leicester when Matt Gillies was promoted to become City's new manager after the sudden exit of David Halliday, then it should not have done.

As a player he had been a calm and thoughtful centre-half who played a key role in the 1954 promotion-winning side.

He found the demands of the First Division a touch out of his reach, and failed to hold down a regular place in the team from then on, eventually playing just 103 League games for the club.

But his ability to understand tactics was obvious, and his interest in coaching saw him receive offers from Italy before he was promoted to Leicester's backroom staff.

He took over the reins when Halliday left, and his impact was such that within two months he had been handed the job on a longer-term basis.

He was a shrewd operator in the transfer market, and an excellent judge of a player – especially when signing a young Gordon Banks before the 1959–60 season for just £7,000. It seemed a lot to pay for a kid that Gillies had spotted in Chesterfield's FA Youth Cup final side three years earlier, but it was a bargain for the man who will always be remembered for the greatest save in England's history against Pelé during the 1970 World Cup.

Gillies was calm and authoritative, and his standing in the community was reflected when he became a justice of the peace.

There were those who said he was too much of a gentleman to be a successful football manager. The next decade was to prove them wrong.

A Taste of
Cup Success

Gillies made an instant impact in his first full season, establishing the club in the top half of the First Division, but also inspiring a run to the FA Cup quarter-finals.

The home tie with the First Division champions Wolves created huge demand for tickets. A record crowd of 22,800 saw a reserve game against Bournemouth in the hope of receiving vouchers to book a place at the match.

These are some of the supporters who were lucky enough to be among the 38,907 who did get in.

The big day finished in disappointment and a 2-1 defeat – indeed just as at Wembley 11 years earlier they were penalized when what looked a good goal was ruled out for a marginal offside decision.

The Leicester public had got the taste for big cup occasions though, and for the next few years they were not going to be disappointed.

LEFT: Disappointed Len Chalmers traipses off after the 2-1 defeat.

BELOW & RIGHT: How the *Daily Mirror* reported the tie.

Goal that sent Leicester hopes soaring

● Bill Slater, Wolves centre half, runs back too late to stop Leicester outside right Tommy McDonald beating Wolves goalkeeper Geoff Sidebottom and scoring his side's only sixth-round goal.

THE SAME STORY 11 YEARS LATER

Leicester 1, Wolves 2

MEMORIES of an eleven-year-old Wembley blow hushed jam-packed Filbert-street in the thirty-eighth minute of this crash-bang sixth round FA Cup clash, writes KEN JONES.

Just a minute after right winger Tommy McDonald had cut Wolves' two-goal lead, inside right Albert Cheesebrough slashed home a left-foot shot past Wolves 'keeper Geoff Sidebottom.

But London linesman Dennis Lewis ruled the goal out for offside . . . and it was a carbon copy incident of the one that robbed burly Ken Chisholm of an equaliser in the 1949 Cup Final in which Wolves beat Leicester 3—1.

I thought that linesman Lewis's flag was up before Cheesebrough put the ball in.

But Leicester players said afterwards: "We thought Albert was onside when he received the ball. And that goal would have made all the difference to us."

But Leicester had already tossed the game away in the first thirty minutes. They stood appealing for offside as Peter Broadbent pounced on an Eddie Clamp pass and crashed home number one.

And right back and skipper Len Chalmers headed into his own goal after a shocking mix-up with 'keeper Gordon Banks.

But this match was Soccer at its lowest. I am convinced that the FA Cup, British football's No. 1 glamour competition, is becoming the game's worst advert.

For the whole ninety minutes it was crash-bang Soccer with hardly one breath of imagination or intelligence to break the monotony of crash tackles and aimless passes.

BELOW: An anxious Gordon Banks watches the action at the other end as Leicester search in vain for an equalizer.

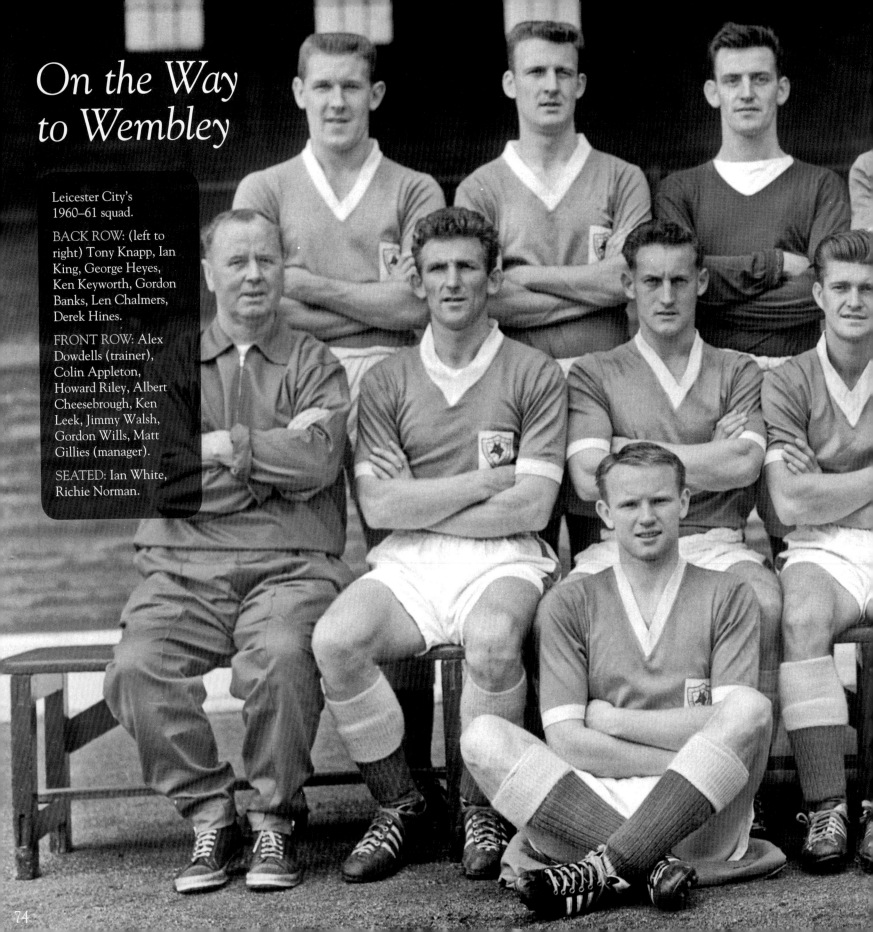

On the Way to Wembley

Leicester City's 1960–61 squad.

BACK ROW: (left to right) Tony Knapp, Ian King, George Heyes, Ken Keyworth, Gordon Banks, Len Chalmers, Derek Hines.

FRONT ROW: Alex Dowdells (trainer), Colin Appleton, Howard Riley, Albert Cheesebrough, Ken Leek, Jimmy Walsh, Gordon Wills, Matt Gillies (manager).

SEATED: Ian White, Richie Norman.

Cup Fever

There was a new buzz around Filbert Street as more than 27,000 saw the first game of a new season, but an opening-day draw with Blackpool turned out to be something of a disappointment.

By the start of September City had slumped to 19th place with just one win from their first six matches and it looked like another relegation struggle was looming.

Instead Matt Gillies made three key signings – Howard Riley, Ken Leek and a young defender called Frank McLintock – and the whole campaign turned around.

By the end of the season Leicester were on course for a sixth-place finish in the First Division, and after beating Sheffield United in an epic semi-final that needed two replays, were heading to Wembley for the season's biggest showpiece.

Leicester's players had become big stars in the city.

Anticipation

Leicester fans take over the car park next to Filbert Street for an impromptu game – maybe in the hope of getting a call-up to Wembley!

RIGHT: The club's mascot tries on his FA Cup final boots.

BELOW: Read all about it – Leicester supporters in the city centre eager for the latest football news.

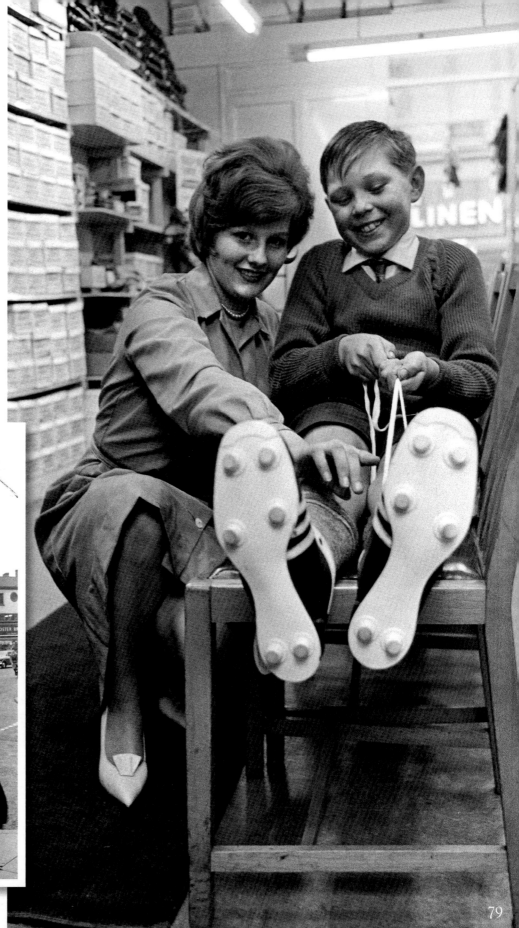

Crowds at one end of Wembley wait for the kick-off.

BELOW: Insight: more than a decade later former Leicester manager John Duncan admits what went wrong with his team's trip to Wembley.

RIGHT: The *Daily Mirror* produced a four-page souvenir pull-out.

When City disobeyed

By JOHNNY DUNCAN

—who managed Leicester's 1949 Cup Final side.

LEICESTER CITY will win the Cup this afternoon . . . if the players pay more attention to manager Matt Gillies than mine did to me twelve years ago.

I had a plan to beat Wolves in 1949. But the lads ignored it. And that's why City are still trying to win the Cup for the first time. Our Final was lost ten minutes after the interval. That was when my "Stop Billy Wright" plan should have gone into action.

BUT IT DIDN'T.

I had noticed in the first half that most of the Wolves danger was coming from Wright, then at left half. Everything, including their two goals, seemed to stem from Billy.

At half-time I drilled into my players that they must try to stop this flow of passes to the Wolves attack.

But our plan went haywire when our right winger Mal Griffiths scored two minutes after the interval. The lads forgot my instructions because they were back in the game.

I don't think Leicester will fail this time. If they can get over the first twenty minutes then they will pull it off.

DAILY MIRROR, Saturday, May 6, 1961. PAGE 13

Mirror Sport 4-PAGE CUP FINAL SOUVENIR

SPURS ARE IN FOR A SHOCK

By FRANK McGHEE

LEICESTER CITY. That is the name of "the other team" at Wembley this afternoon. You may have forgotten—and you can be forgiven if you had. They have been dismissed to an extent that would make most teams either nervous wrecks or recklessly angry, ripe candidates for defeat.

LEICESTER CITY ARE NEITHER.

Leicester City are quietly assured about the role many people have decided in advance will be theirs this afternoon . . .

Glamour

Cocky

His big day

Fiercer

Speed kills!

—says BILL HOLDEN

LINE-UP OF THE TEAMS, TELE-VISION AND RADIO DETAILS ARE ON THE BACK OF THIS FOUR-PAGE PULL-OUT.

The Double-Winners

After all the excitement of the preparation, Leicester found themselves just a footnote in history as Danny Blanchflower held aloft the FA Cup to confirm Tottenham as the first winners in the 20th Century of the League and FA Cup Double.

Manager Matt Gillies sprung a huge surprise by dropping Ken Leek, who had scored in every previous round, but the real turning point came when full-back Len Chalmers suffered a serious knee injury early in the first half.

He carried on bravely but was really only a passenger on the wing. With effectively only 10 men, City held out until the 66th minute when Bobby Smith scored, and later, with just 14 minutes remaining, a Terry Dyson header settled the game.

The moment Leicester's chances
were effectively ended when Len
Chalmers injured his knee.

ABOVE: Spurs celebrate Terry Dyson's goal.

LEFT: The old baths at Wembley are a scene for celebration.

BELOW: A historic double – Danny Blanchflower is lifted with the FA Cup.

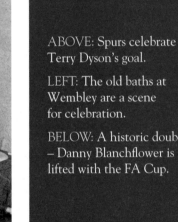

● Fourteen minutes to go—the 'double' is in the bag!

● Leicester 'keeper Gordon Banks is beaten by a bullet of a header from Terry Dyson (out of picture) . . . and Spurs are 2—0 up, with fourteen minutes to go.

WRECKED—BY THE OLD MEN!

"WELL — they won, but. . . ." Those four words, spoken by the man next to me at Wembley as referee Kelly blew his whistle for the last time, summed up yet another basically unsatisfactory Cup Final.

KEVAN IS BACK FOR ENGLAND

By KEN JONES

Peter Wilson
—AT THE CUP FINAL

A hand from the Mayor

Herd ill —misses victory

From JIMMY STEVENSON
Dublin, Sunday.

83

–LEGENDS–

Frank McLintock

When Matt Gillies took over as manager, his big advantage was that as a player and then a coach he knew every detail of the staff he had inherited.

That included a raw, lean and lanky, but rock-hard kid who had been brought down from the Gorbals in Glasgow in 1957 and made a huge impression in Leicester's reserve teams.

It was actually previous boss David Halliday who had given Frank McLintock his debut as an 18-year-old in the last days of his reign, but he didn't have the confidence to keep him in the team. Gillies picked him and made him one of the linchpins of the side.

He was an essential part of the team which reached two FA Cup finals and won the Football League Cup in 1964. Although undoubtedly a tough tackler, he also had a superb touch when passing the ball and could create far more than he destroyed.

When City sold him to Arsenal for a club record £80,000 early in the 1964–65 season he had already been capped by Scotland, and the only surprise was that he didn't win more international honours as he went on to become as vital at Highbury as he had been at Filbert Street.

FOOTBALL –STATS–

Frank McLintock

Name: Francis McLintock

Born: December 1939

Playing career: 1957–77

Clubs: Leicester City, Arsenal, Queens Park Rangers

Leicester appearances: 200

Goals: 28

Scotland appearances: 9

Goals: 1

–LEGENDS–

Ken Keyworth

Another of David Halliday's astute signings, Ken Keyworth, had arrived from his home town of Rotherham for just £9,000 – although his record of barely six goals in 87 League games for the Yorkshire side hardly marked him out as a prolific forward.

He took time to establish himself with City as well, scoring just three goals in 20 games in his first season of regular first-team football. But a switch to a deeper role the following year transformed his career and was yet another example of the ability of Gillies to find potential in players that other coaches could not see.

He was the club's top scorer for three seasons in a row, netting 27 goals in his best campaign of 1962–63, including one at Wembley when City reached another FA Cup final.

Disappointingly he never quite regained his form or confidence after being involved in a car accident not long after a starring performance in both legs of the 1964 League Cup final, and was released to Coventry on a free transfer.

FOOTBALL –STATS–

Ken Keyworth

Name: Ken Keyworth

Born: February 1934

Died: January 2000

Playing career: 1955–65

Clubs: Rotherham United, Leicester City, Coventry City, Swindon

Leicester appearances: 215

Goals: 76

French referee is under fire from the fans

LEICESTER TAME THE SPANIARDS

By PETER INGALL.

Leicester 1, Atletico Madrid 1

FRENCH referee Pierre Schwinte was loudly booed for a decision which robbed Leicester of what looked to be a perfect goal.

It happened in the eighteenth minute of this second-round European Cup-winners' competition, and put the home crowd in an angry mood.

Inside left Colin Appleton pushed a good pass through to Ken Keyworth, and the inside right held off a late challenge before hitting the ball into the net.

To the amazement of the crowd and his linesman, the referee gave a free kick against the Spaniards for a foul on Appleton.

This strange decision brought unnecessary feeling into the game, and both sides, particularly Madrid, were guilty of tough tackles.

Leicester played well, producing quick-moving football that upset the Madrid defence.

In fact, Madrid, second in the Spanish League, were at times so much in a tangle that it was a good job goalkeeper Egardo Madinabeytia was in good form. He made several fine saves.

Pretty

Madrid played some pretty stuff, but City's goalkeeper, Gordon Banks, who arrived only forty minutes before the start—he was reserve at Wembley—was troubled only once.

That was when right half Rodin Ramiro let fly a twenty - five - yard shot which Banks tipped over

After surviving more hard tackles in which centre forward Gordon Wills and Keyworth were injured, Leicester took the lead in the fifty-seventh minute with a great goal.

Appleton sent a long pass out to right winger Howard Riley, who beat three men before pulling the ball back for a dazed Keyworth to slam into the net.

With only seconds to go centre forward Jorge Mendoza scored a shock equaliser.

Leicester go to Madrid in three weeks' time for the second leg and, on this showing, must stand a good chance of reaching the next round. Every man was a hero.

Leicester crash in Cup

Madrid, Wednesday.

Atletico 2, Leicester 0

(Atletico win 3—1 on aggregate)

LEICESTER, the team standing in for double champions Spurs, were knocked out of the European Cup winners' cup here tonight.

Atletico go through for the the quarter-finals, having drawn 1—1 at Leicester in the first leg last month.

It was a defeat with humiliation for a Leicester team, who could manage only one shot to test the Spanish goalkeeper.

Leicester looked second-raters as the Madrid side —they are second in the Spanish League— mastered every move.

Atletico scored through Collar (penalty) and Jones in the second half.

A European Adventure

The 1961 FA Cup final might have ended in disappointment but there was one consolation for Leicester – Tottenham's status as Double winners meant that a place in the European Cup Winners' Cup was up for grabs.

The first-round draw was less than glamorous – in fact it was still in Britain because Leicester were paired against Northern Ireland side Glenavon. But a thumping 7-2 aggregate win against the part-timers was rewarded with a second-round tie against Spanish giants Atlético Madrid.

More than 25,000 were at Filbert Street for the club's first taste of competitive European football. Goalkeeper Gordon Banks had to make a dash from Wembley where he had been reserve for an England match in the afternoon against Portugal, and arrived with just 40 minutes to spare.

And though Leicester felt that an early Ken Keyworth goal should not have been disallowed, there was joy when another Keyworth effort did stand.

The Spaniards scrambled a late equalizer, however, and were then far too good in the second leg and Leicester's brief adventure was ended all too soon.

A more permanent status in the First Division allowed manager Matt Gillies to start improving the club's infrastructure – and among his ideas was to vary the training methods.

For a while that meant coach trips to a nearby indoor sports hall to play badminton as a way of breaking up the routine while still maintaining sharpness.

Stepping Out

Football in the 1960s was still a far cry from today's game where sports science is at the fore, but ideas on fitness training were developing.

Matt Gillies was earning a reputation as a forward thinker, and introduced ideas on exercises for greater flexibility.

LEFT: Forwards (from left) Howard Riley, Graham Cross, Ken Keyworth, David Gibson and Mike Stringfellow are seen trying out a Tiller Girls-style high-stepping routine during a Filbert Street training session in 1963.

The Nearly Season

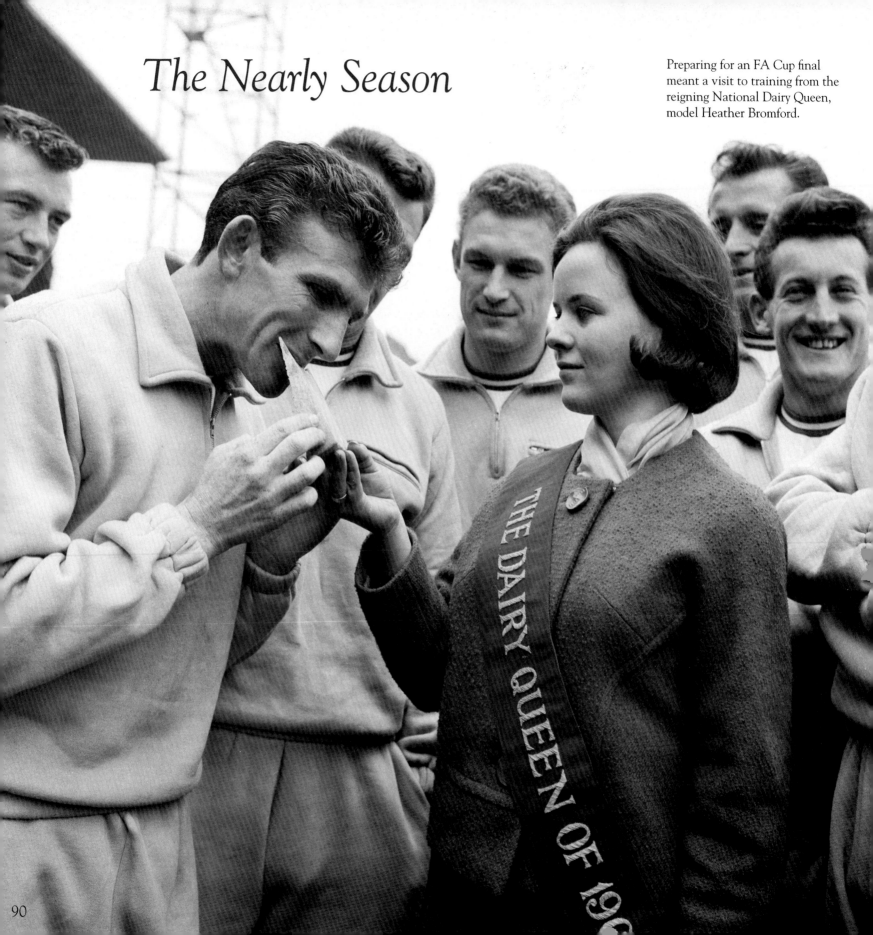

Preparing for an FA Cup final meant a visit to training from the reigning National Dairy Queen, model Heather Bromford.

Two years after watching Spurs celebrate their unique Double, Leicester had the chance to achieve the same feat.

A 4-3 win over Manchester United at the end of April saw them go to the top of the First Division table, and then Mike Stringfellow's goal in the FA Cup semi-final against Liverpool at Hillsborough was enough to earn Leicester another trip to Wembley.

Sadly the League campaign fell away as Leicester lost their final four matches to eventually finish fourth, but there were still high hopes as they faced Manchester United on FA Cup final day.

ABOVE: The teams walk out at Wembley.

BELOW: Leicester's players are introduced to Prince Philip.

Wembley Woes

After seeing their League form collapse, Leicester hoped they could rediscover their sparkle on FA Cup final day. But though they came close to taking an early lead, a piece of brilliance by Denis Law after 33 minutes (main picture) put United in front.

David Herd got a second, and though Ken Keyworth briefly raised hopes with a header, a rare mistake by Gordon Banks presented Herd with his second of the day and United were destined to collect the silverware.

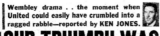

PETER WILSON   One-man Final —Denis had a dream day

Oh, the majesty of the Law . .

DENIS LAW . . . "never a foot wrong, never a moment when he wasn't the inspiration of Manchester, and the lash for Leicester."

Wembley drama . . the moment when United could easily have crumbled into a ragged rabble—reported by KEN JONES.

CUP TRIUMPH WAS SO NEAR TRAGEDY

Manchester Utd 3, Leicester City 1

The agony of skipper Cantwell

TINY BOROUGH GO FOR THE BIG-TIME

By TOM LYONS

PLAYBOY!

League Cup Winners

After so many near misses, Leicester finally collected a trophy when they won the Football League Cup in 1964.

The competition was still in its infancy, with the final played over two legs.

Gordon Banks made up for his costly error at Wembley the previous season by producing two of his finest performances. He kept a fluent Stoke side at bay in the first leg at the Victoria Ground, and then made a series of stunning saves as Leicester won the next game 3-2 thanks to goals from Mike Stringfellow, David Gibson and Howard Riley.

BELOW: Gordon Banks collects the ball to snuff out danger in the second leg at Filbert Street.

ABOVE: A flying save at Stoke.

BELOW: Banks in the thick of the action again at Stoke, helped by right-back Len Chalmers.

LEICESTER SNATCH THE LEAGUE CUP FROM BRAVE STOKE

By PETER INGALL: Leicester 3, Stoke 2

LEICESTER CITY last night became the third Midland club to win the League Cup—on a 4—3 aggregate—and both teams were cheered to the echo after this Filbert-street thriller.

The man that Leicester had to thank for this success was goalkeeper Gordon Banks, who produced his best England form.

He brought off three fantastic saves from centre forward John Ritchie.

Leicester took a deserved lead in the sixth minute when left winger Mike Stringfellow bamboozled his way past two defenders to score a fine goal.

Inspired by skipper Palmer and the clever promptings of inside left Jimmy McIlroy, Stoke stormed back.

And three minutes after the interval, inside right Dennis Viollet got a clever equaliser.

Then Palmer was carried off the field with an ankle injury.

He returned fifteen minutes later to see inside right David Gibson give Leicester the lead

Leicester made certain when outside right Howard Riley scored the third goal, but still Stoke hit back.

With seconds to go, the limping Palmer put over a centre for centre half George Kinnell to side-foot the ball home

A League Cup Near Miss

Nobody could accuse City of taking the defence of their first major trophy lightly.

They battled through replays with Peterborough and Crystal Palace as well as putting out Grimsby and Coventry before John Sjoberg's goal in the second leg of the semi-final against Plymouth secured a final date with Chelsea.

Luck ran out for Leicester though amid first-leg drama at Filbert Street as Gordon Banks broke his nose in a collision early in the game with George Graham – and bravely played on only to break a thumb in the second half.

Chelsea edged that tie 3-2, and then despite a huge effort by City's forwards at Stamford Bridge, they held on to secure a 0-0 draw and collect the trophy.

Gordon Banks in action at Filbert Street – he broke his nose and a thumb in the game.

ABOVE & BELOW: Action from the first leg.

RIGHT: Terry Venables holds the League Cup trophy after Chelsea's second-leg success.

–LEGENDS–

Gordon Banks

The man who became England's greatest goalkeeper was a raw 17-year-old when Matt Gillies decided to spend a night watching the 1956 FA Youth Cup final at nearby Chesterfield.

Gillies saw evidence of a massive talent that night, and three years later returned to buy Gordon Banks for just £7,000.

It represented a gamble, but it was one which paid off handsomely for both club and eventually country as the calm young man with the solid style emerged as arguably the world's greatest goalkeeper.

Brilliant in the FA Cup runs of 1961 and 1963 (despite a mistake in the final), he was also the rock on which the 1964 League Cup victory was founded and spread confidence throughout the team.

He made his England debut in 1963 as Alf Ramsey looked for ways to build a side ahead of the 1966 World Cup. Banks was soon established as the first-choice keeper and enjoyed the finest moment of his magnificent career at Wembley on 30th July 1966 as captain Bobby Moore lifted the Jules Rimet trophy.

Banks the brave collects the ball at the feet of Spurs legend Jimmy Greaves.

Safe hands – Banks in training gathering the ball between team-mates John Sjoberg and Ian King (above), and working on his own (below).

FOOTBALL -STATS-

Gordon Banks

Name: Gordon Banks

Born: December 1937

Playing career: 1958–78

Clubs: Chesterfield, Leicester City, Stoke City, Fort Lauderdale Strikers

Leicester appearances: 356

England appearances: 73

ABOVE LEFT: Banks with team-mates on an outing to a nearby golf store.

ABOVE: Banks with team-mate Richie Norman autographing a cricket bat.

LEFT: Frank McLintock, Colin Appleton and Banks celebrate with team-mates after all three had just become fathers.

World Cup Winner

As Banks returned to Filbert Street a hero, it was impossible to imagine that less than a year later he would have been moved on. But by April 1967 another brilliant young goalkeeper called Peter Shilton was emerging through the ranks. Manager Matt Gillies made the tough decision to cash in by accepting a £50,000 offer from Stoke and so make room for the prodigy.

Banks of England – Gordon in action during the World Cup final.

ABOVE: Even in victory it is typical of the modest style of Leicester's great that he is just visible in the background (third left) in the most iconic image of English football's greatest day.

BELOW: Time off – Banks reads a newspaper while the rest of England's 1966 players enjoy a game of cards at the team hotel.

-LEGENDS-

John Sjoberg

Aberdeen-born John Sjoberg was another recruit found by the club's successful scouting operations in Scotland.

Watched after playing for Scottish Schools against their English counterparts at Wembley, he was 19 when he made his City debut, becoming a regular first-team player in time to earn a place in the 1963 FA Cup final side.

His versatility meant he could switch from full-back to the centre of defence with ease, and his strength in the air helped him establish a centre-back pairing with Graham Cross which became the mainstay of Leicester's side for seven seasons.

ABOVE: Mike Stringfellow gets in front of former Leicester star Frank McLintock to try a shot at goal in a game at Arsenal.

BELOW: John Sjoberg beats Aston Villa's Derek Dougan (later to play for Leicester) in a heading duel.

FOOTBALL -STATS-

John Sjoberg

Name: John Sjoberg

Born: June 1941

Died: October 2008

Playing career: 1958–73

Clubs: Leicester City, Rotherham United

Leicester appearances: 413

Goals: 19

—LEGENDS—

Mike Stringfellow

Mike Stringfellow's first appearance at Filbert Street was as a skinny 17-year-old for Mansfield in a League Cup tie, with a performance so dazzling that Matt Gillies was determined to buy him.

The Stags turned down several bids before accepting a British record £25,000 fee for a teenager in 1962.

He scored 19 goals in his first full season, including the header against Liverpool which won the FA Cup semi-final of 1963.

His crosses from the left wing provided consistent ammunition for City's forwards, and it was a shame that in the early 1970s the toll of being kicked by desperate full-backs began to show itself in a succession of injuries which limited his later appearances.

He is the only player after Arthur Chandler to be in the top 10 for both appearances and goals.

FOOTBALL —STATS—

Mike Stringfellow

Name: Michael David Stringfellow

Born: January 1943

Playing career: 1960–75

Clubs: Mansfield Town, Leicester City

Leicester appearances: 370

Goals: 97

—LEGENDS—

Graham Cross

A player who was ahead of his time, Graham Cross had the ability to switch from defence to midfield and prove just as effective in any position – he was later used as an emergency centre-forward, too.

It was on his 18th birthday that he first shone, picked to play at centre-half against Atlético Madrid in City's European Cup Winners' Cup adventure.

From there the man nicknamed 'The Tank' played countless games with both power and finesse on the ball.

He ended up just short of Adam Black's record for Football League appearances, but City's exploits in both the FA Cup and League Cup during his time made him the club's all-time appearance record holder with a total of 599 – a figure unlikely ever to be beaten.

Just to further prove his ability as an all-rounder, he also played county cricket for Leicestershire for 16 years, scoring more than 2,000 first-class runs and taking 92 wickets.

FOOTBALL —STATS—

Graham Cross

Name: Graham Frederick Cross

Born: November 1943

Playing career: 1960–79

Clubs: Leicester City, Chesterfield, Brighton, Preston, Lincoln

Leicester appearances: 599

Goals: 37

Graham Cross, who played a total of 599 games for Leicester City.

A New Era

After a decade of success, Matt Gillies might have expected some support when he hit his first bad patch at the start of the 1968–69 season.

Instead, with Leicester bottom of the table in December, the board chose to sack his trusted coach Bert Johnson and Gillies resigned in protest.

Needing a quick replacement, City's directors looked at the growing reputation of former West Ham wing-half Frank O'Farrell who had enjoyed success first at Weymouth, then Torquay.

He couldn't stave off the threat of relegation – Leicester finished 21st – but he did inspire a superb FA Cup run which meant that a decade which began with a Wembley appearance was to end the same way.

Frank O'Farrell at work on the training ground.

'Sniffer' Finds a Golden Goal

One of the last big transfer deals done by Matt Gillies was to pay a club record £150,000 to Fulham for proven goalscorer Allan Clarke.

It was a move which didn't bring instant success in the League, where he got just a dozen goals as City slid towards the Second Division, but he was most certainly the man for the big occasion.

His eight FA Cup strikes included the semi-final winner against West Bromwich Albion at Hillsborough.

ABOVE: The boot that won a semi-final – Allan Clarke after the game.

RIGHT: An injury scare – Frank O'Farrell looks on as Clarke receives treatment.

ABOVE: Moment of joy – Clarke celebrates the winning goal against West Brom.

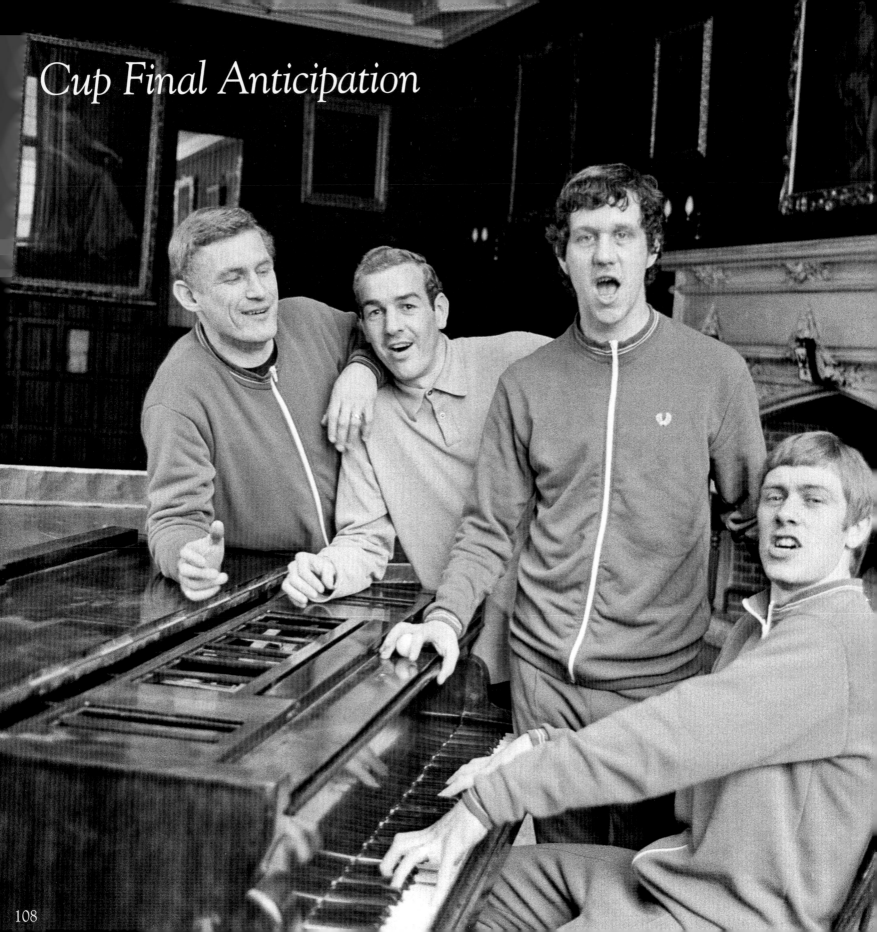

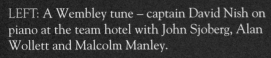

LEFT: A Wembley tune – captain David Nish on piano at the team hotel with John Sjoberg, Alan Wollett and Malcolm Manley.

RIGHT: Newspaper cuttings: how the *Daily Mirror* saw the line-ups.

BELOW RIGHT: Princess Anne shakes hands with Len Glover as she is introduced to Leicester's team at Wembley.

After two FA Cup final defeats in the previous eight years, and the threat of relegation which was hanging over the remaining five League games, Leicester fans set off to Wembley full of optimism with memories of a 3-0 win over Manchester City earlier that season.

More Wembley Woe

Leicester's FA Cup luck remained out – a mixture of injuries to key players and missed chances in front of goal meant Joe Mercer's Manchester City collected the silverware.

ABOVE: Peter Shilton comes out to make a save . . .

LEFT: . . . but he can do nothing to stop Neil Young scoring and the Manchester City players celebrate his 24th-minute winning goal.

RIGHT: What might have been: the *Daily Mirror*'s verdict on the final.

BELOW: The reality of what was to come next for Leicester.

LEICESTER LIMP HOME

Four players injured for match they must win . .

By KEN JONES

LEICESTER CITY have less than forty-eight hours to repair the damage done to their pride and their players in Saturday's F A Cup Final.

They need to hit championship form if they are to avoid relegation from the First Division, and they could be without three of their Cup Final team when they meet Spurs at home tomorrow night.

Left winger Len Glover, who limped off in the 68th minute, has no chance of playing. In fact, it's likely that Glover and centre half John Sjoberg, who missed the Final through injury, could be out for the season.

Allan Clarke, voted Wembley's "Man of the Match," and Bobby Roberts are also doubtful for a game Leicester must win. And Leicester manager Frank O'Farrell says:

We are facing what is probably the most important period in the club's history. I have said for weeks that our season would begin when the Final was over, and that still stands.

Reserves

These injuries could not have come at a worse time, and we may have to rely on reserve men Brian Greenhalgh and Paul Matthews. The Spurs match is more important even than the Cup Final because we have got to show that we have the ability to come back.

The programme could hardly be tougher. If we can take seven points from our remaining five games we can stay up—and that would be the sort of form that wins championships.

I'm taking the team away for twenty-four hours so we can get together and talk the Final out of our system. We mustn't shed any tears. The players did all that was humanly possible and proved we were not the pushovers people expected.

The general opinion before the game was that we were there only to make up the number but it didn't work out that way. We had our chances and I'm sure that if we had equalised in the second half we would have won.

Decisive

Our performance should give us confidence. It has certainly made me feel that we can survive. We won a lot of friends at Wembley and the players know they weren't disgraced or outclassed by Manchester City.

Every match will now be decisive, and none of them easy. All along, the whole thing has been time, I'm sure that if the bad weather hadn't interrupted a good run earlier in the year we would not be in this desperate position.

But on Saturday it was the old story. Our goals column speaks for itself. We have scored only nine away from home and three of those came in one match at Sheffield Wednesday.

When I looked at the two teams on Saturday I considered that Manchester City have had four years to create their style. You see, it is time that matters.

Leeds United have taken time to get where they are and Leicester need more time to establish themselves. That's why it's important we stay in the First Division.

Leicester's programme is formidable. After the Spurs match they go to Ipswich on Saturday and then play Sunderland and Everton at home and Manchester United away in little over a week.

Adventure

They showed in the final they have the character to stay up, but it is their skills and particularly their finishing which will be severely tested now.

Manchester City achieved the target, but the style which won them the Cup will be more realistic next season.

Sad as it may seem to the purists. Manchester City are forced to accept that ideals must be sacrificed to a certain extent in the cause of continued success.

Like West Ham their weakness has been the adventure in their play. They make so much room for themselves to go forward that they leave room in which their opponents can play.

Manager Joe Mercer says: "There is one side of the game when you stretch a defence by attacking. We are good at this. But there is another when you have to contract and play containing football.

"Leeds United are the best in the game at this. They are as enthusiastic going forwards as the best going backwards as they are going forwards.

We do not intend to sacrifice our good points. We want the best of both worlds. We must learn to control a game.

Manchester City were unable to do this in the Final despite Mike Summerbee's early domination of Leicester's left flank and the goal which came from his beautifully judged pass to Neil Young in the twenty-third minute.

Summerbee ran with skill and determination in that opening spell. But he faded from the game. Francis Lee and Tony Coleman were also unable to make a sustained contribution to City's football.

Memorable

If Peter Rodrigues and Len Glover had taken chances made by the astute David Gibson the game could easily have turned against the betting. As I expected, Leicester's passing improved at Wembley but the best of it was all in the first half, and then it fell away at a vital stage of the game.

It was a worthwhile Final, memorable for Manchester City's composed passing and Leicester's combative attitude.

A Book at bath-time . .

Manchester captain Tony Book relaxes in the bath after City's Wembley triumph . . . and the F A Cup comes in handy to rinse the soap out of his hair.

MANCHESTER CITY	. . . : . : . .	1
Young (24 min)		
LEICESTER CITY	. . . . : . : . .	0
Att : 100,000	Receipts : £128,000	

Hard luck, son ..

Manchester City manager Joe Mercer knows all about the heartaches of the Cup . . . and his first move at the end of the match was to console Leicester skipper David Nish.
Picture: MONTE FRESCO

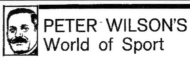
IF ONLY ANDY HADN'T MISSED!

IF the players had been able to keep up the pace and elan with which they started, it could have been one of the most memorable of all Cup Finals.

Instead — physical stamina and human memory being what they are—the recollection is of a series of exciting light-cavalry charges degenerating into the tired trudging of exhausted infantry in the last quarter of an hour.

Immortal

So for me it will not be as Technicolored a memory as the immortal 4—3 win that Blackpool scored over Bolton sixteen years ago.

Or, although undoubtedly the better side won, as dramatically satisfying as Manchester United's electrifying performance six years ago; when Leicester City were again left defeated.

To me the turning point at Wembley on Saturday came some seven minutes after the change-over.

Had Leicester's Andy Lochhead, quite unmenaced by any defender, then rammed home an equaliser like a musket ball safely stowed into a Brown Bess, the whole complexion of the game might have been turned topsy-turvy.

Tiring

Few men get such a chance in our greatest domestic match; no man deserves two such opportunities.

Although there were other alarums and excursions in the remaining time, I never thought Manchester City would lose after this.

Yet it was Manchester who tired the first and more obviously. Much has been written of the deterioration of the Wembley turf. But it still seems to exert its strength - sapping effect

ANDY LOCHHEAD . . . He missed the chance to equalise for Leicester and perhaps turn the Wembley Final topsy-turvy.

on even the fittest athletes.

Despite the inexhaustible spirit of Tony Book, the brilliance of Mike Summerbee—which paled after the first twenty-five minutes—the danger of Colin Bell, and the panther prowls of Neil Young, plus the diligence of Allan Clarke, you could see the strength draining out of player after player like sugar from a split sack.

In the end it was as though the "failing sickness" had spread through the field like an epidemic.

I can only think that referee George McCabe must be the first chairman of the imaginary Society for the Prevention of Cruelty to Players.

By my stop-watch he allowed only fifteen seconds of injury time, whereas the true period must have been closer to five minutes.

Conclusion

However, it seemed as though the conclusion had actually been arrived at long before.

So criticism should be tempered with forbearance, and in retrospect this will remain a good, professional final, but not a great, pulse-stirring event to remember.

ITV man claims: I lost a tooth in battle to interview players after the big game

BBC IS ACCUSED OVER CUP TV FIGHT

By DAVID WRIGHT

AN ITV floor manager claimed yesterday that he was "attacked" by a B B C man in the "battle of Wembley" between T V crews at the Cup Final.

David Yallop, 31, said he was jumped on and hit. He lost a tooth—and ended the match bruised and battered.

In tears.. Nish, the losing captain

A tear or two . . David Nish, Leicester's captain, yesterday.

DE GAULLE FACES DEFEAT

RECORD WIN FOR JACKIE

Income Tax

many people pay more than they have to

Action

Police close a freak-out church

RIGHT: It seems that Leicester v Man City wasn't the only battle going on at Wembley!

113

The Long Road Back

Relegation after a decade of life in the top flight was a major blow, but O'Farrell was determined to mount a promotion campaign.

He brought his players back early for pre-season fitness work – which in those days meant endless running up the hills of the Leicestershire countryside.

Behind the Scenes

Frank O'Farrell's time at West Ham had left him heavily influenced by the coaching ideas of Ron Greenwood, and players like Malcolm Allison who had nurtured the idea of the Hammers' academy, which also turned men like John Bond, Ken Brown and Noel Cantwell into top managers.

   With another ex-Hammer, Malcolm Musgrove as his coach, they set about rebuilding the team to chase a return. That meant not only signing new players but improvements behind the scenes – taking over an indoor training centre to help combat the weather.

ABOVE: Leicester's indoor soccer hall.

ABOVE: A rest between training sessions.

BELOW: Improved medical facilities – Len Glover and Peter Rodrigues on the treatment tables.

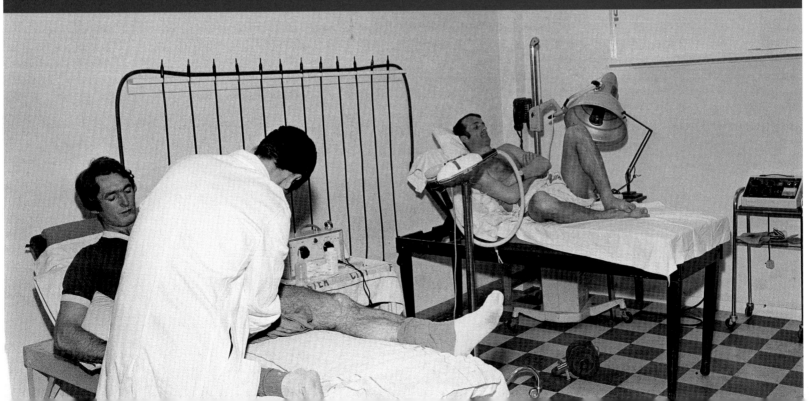

The Entertainers
1970-1979

All shook up! Frank Worthington, a master entertainer on the pitch, did Elvis impressions at a local club when away from his footballing duties.

The professionals: Keith Weller and Alan Birchenall dressed as 1970s TV characters Bodie and Doyle.

1970 Missed out on promotion by two points. **1971** Promoted as Second Division champions; Frank O'Farrell leaves to take over Manchester United; Jimmy Bloomfield appointed manager. **1972** Strip changed to all white for a season. **1974** FA Cup semifinal v Liverpool. **1975** Graham Cross suspended for playing cricket for Leicestershire. **1976** Executive boxes built at Filbert Street. **1977** Jimmy Bloomfield resigns; replacement Frank McLintock lasts only one season which ends in relegation. **1978** Jock Wallace takes over. **1979** Keith Weller wears white tights in a televised FA Cup game.

Promotion – and Change

Frank O'Farrell's first season ended in a near miss, just two points away from promotion, but the next season's superb defending – which saw only 30 goals conceded – helped clinch the Second Division Championship.

Within weeks of celebrating that success, however, O'Farrell had accepted an offer to take over at Manchester United following the retirement of Sir Matt Busby.

In his place Leicester's board appointed Jimmy Bloomfield, whose career as an imaginative inside-forward had been followed by success with Leyton Orient in his first management job.

Jimmy Bloomfield signs autographs, tries out the manager's office, and holds a training session after taking charge in the summer of 1971.

Charity (Shield) Begins at Home

Bloomfield's reign began with a trophy. The 1971 Double winners Arsenal had chosen not to contest the FA Charity Shield, and the FA decided the traditional curtain-raiser to the season should be between the Second Division champions and the FA Cup runners-up.

The match was held at Filbert Street, and a crowd of more than 25,000 saw Steve Whitworth score the game's only goal. For Bloomfield it was a perfect start and raised hopes of more to come.

LEFT: Rodney Fern and Steve Whitworth celebrate the winning goal.

BELOW: Liverpool's Ray Clemence saves from John Farrington.

BELOW: Graham Cross heads clear.

London Lads

Leicester's promotion-winning players were in for a shock as Bloomfield set about rebuilding the team almost as soon as he took over.

His brief was to construct an entertaining, attacking team and he wasted no time reaching for the cheque book to sign Jon Sammels from his old club Arsenal for £100,000.

There were more Cockney accents to join the dressing room. Keith Weller came from Chelsea for the same six-figure fee, and Alan Birchenall arrived on the same day in October from Crystal Palace who got £45,000 plus Bobby Kellard in return.

Just as big a sign of ambition was turning down a bid of £175,000 from Derby for goalkeeper Peter Shilton, and an even bigger offer from Arsenal.

It brought a 12th-place finish in Bloomfield's first season in charge, and a growing reputation for playing football with flair.

LEFT: Time for tea . . . Clarice Laxton serves a welcoming cuppa to Jon Sammels, Alan Birchenall, Keith Weller, Len Glover, Dennis Rofe and Jimmy Bloomfield.

BELOW: Game for a laugh . . . Weller and Birchenall in another pose made famous by the TV series *The Professionals*.

125

The Balloon Goes Up

It wasn't only on the field that Leicester were becoming adventurous – under Bloomfield's guidance they were keen to be up to date with modern technology, too.

One big investment designed to guarantee that matches and training could beat the winter weather was a giant balloon which covered the entire Filbert Street pitch.

It was big enough to play a full training match underneath and also enabled the groundsman to carry out his maintenance regardless of the conditions outside.

All White on the Night

Bloomfield's revolutionary ideas included throwing out nearly a century of tradition by changing the home kit from blue to all white.

His rather peculiar reasoning was that it made the players look bigger and more fearsome – an idea that didn't go down well with fans. Within a year the traditional colours had been restored and white remained only in use as a change strip.

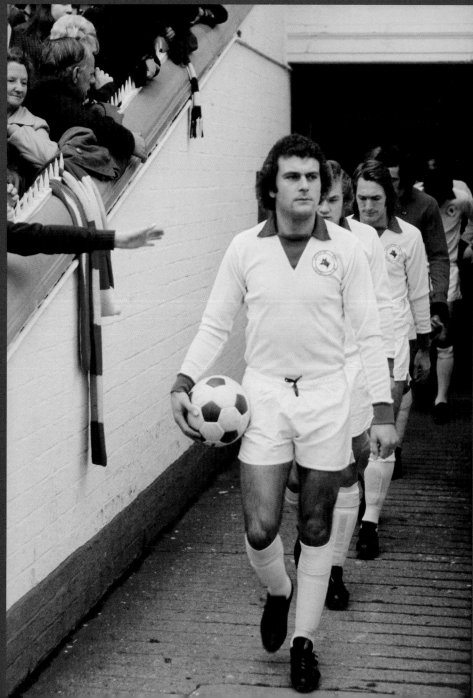

A Heavyweight Boss

Leicester's success was gaining the manager a growing media profile, and he saw that as a way of further building the club's 1970s image as an exciting and progressive outfit.

These pictures were taken for a special *Daily Mirror* feature on him in 1974.

–LEGENDS–

Alan Birchenall

Jimmy Bloomfield loved to have big characters in his dressing room, and few were as much fun as Alan Birchenall.

Modern fans have known him since 1983 as the club's effervescent PR man, but there was exactly the same dash of showmanship about the way he played, whether as a forward, winger or in midfield.

His arrival with Keith Weller was one of the key moments of the 1971–72 season, and for the following six years he was as vital a part of the club on the field as he is nowadays off of it. His goal tally of just 14 in that time hardly does credit to his contribution. If they had kept statistics in those days for assists it would have been much easier to look back at the depth of his talent.

RIGHT: Beating Bobby Moore to the ball.

FOOTBALL
-STATS-

Alan Birchenall

Name: Alan John Birchenall

Born: August 1945

Playing career: 1963–83

Clubs: Sheffield United, Chelsea, Crystal Palace, Leicester City, San Jose Earthquakes, Notts County, Memphis Rogues, Blackburn Rovers, Luton, Hereford

Leicester appearances: 183
Goals: 14

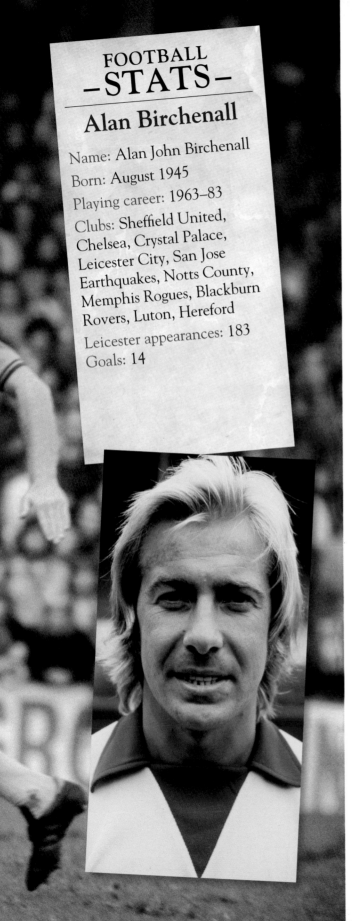

LEFT: With bags packed as he heads from London to Leicester with wife Heather and daughter Laura.

BELOW: Teammates: Birchenall with Frank Worthington and manager Jimmy Bloomfield.

Togetherness

Jon Sammels, Malcolm Munro, Len Glover, Steve Earle and Steve Whitworth celebrate Earle's second goal in a 1974 FA Cup win against Oxford.

ABOVE & BELOW: Dennis Rofe, manager Jimmy Bloomfield, Frank Worthington, Peter Shilton and Keith Weller with the Filbert Street balloon in the background.

The 1974–75 squad.

BACK ROW: (left to right) Dennis Rofe, Alan Woollett, Pat Kruse, Carl Jayes, Steve Yates, David Tomlin, Steve Earle, Joe Waters.

MIDDLE ROW: David Coates (coach), Mike Stringfellow, Bob Lee, Mark Wallington, Peter Shilton, Malcolm Partridge, Malcolm Munro, George Preston (physio).

FRONT ROW: Len Glover, Graham Cross, Steve Whitworth, John Smith (secretary), Jimmy Bloomfield (manager), Keith Weller, Frank Worthington, Alan Birchenall, Jon Sammels.

–LEGENDS–

Peter Shilton

Filbert Street legend says it was Gordon Banks who first noticed the talent of a young boy playing for Leicester Schools and suggested he should be singled out for special coaching.

Within a few years it was to rebound on the England goalkeeper as his prodigy not only forced his departure from Filbert Street, but also meant he had discovered his England goalkeeping successor.

Hugely determined and ambitious, Shilton made his debut when he was just 16, keeping a clean sheet against Everton, and within a year manager Matt Gillies had to decide whether to let him go to one of the list of First Division clubs wanting to sign him, or cash in on World Cup-winner Banks instead.

He chose to stick with the youngster, and Leicester were rewarded with more than 300 appearances in which they could always rely on Shilton's agility to produce a brilliant save when needed.

He was eventually reunited with Banks at Stoke as Leicester struggled to give him a trophy-winning team to support his ambition – Jimmy Bloomfield accepting a bid of £325,000.

His eventual record-breaking England career of 125 caps owed everything to his dedication. He could be argued to have been the man who set the standard in his profession, turning the art of goalkeeping into a science of angles, analysis and positioning.

RIGHT: The master of his six-yard box, Shilton barks orders to the defence.

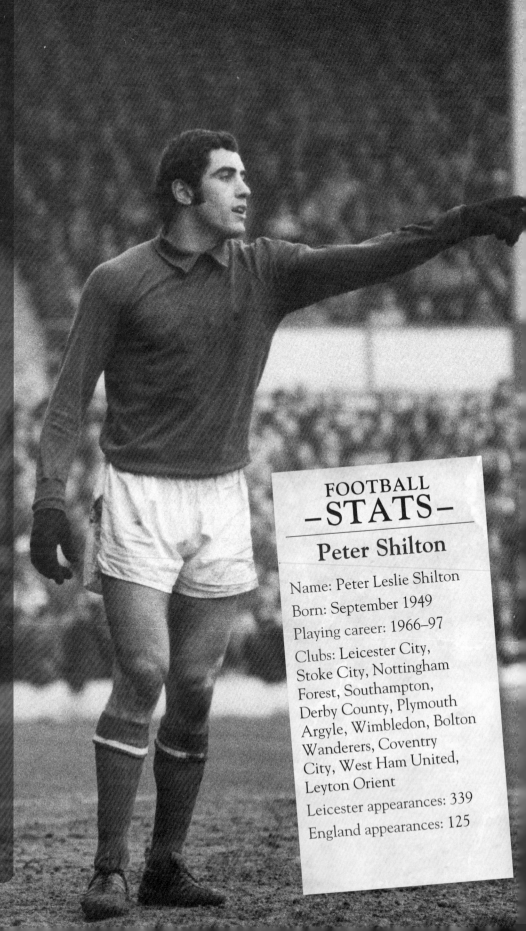

FOOTBALL –STATS–

Peter Shilton

Name: Peter Leslie Shilton

Born: September 1949

Playing career: 1966–97

Clubs: Leicester City, Stoke City, Nottingham Forest, Southampton, Derby County, Plymouth Argyle, Wimbledon, Bolton Wanderers, Coventry City, West Ham United, Leyton Orient

Leicester appearances: 339

England appearances: 125

The secret was always hard work on the training ground.

LEFT: Another spectacular save.

RIGHT: Proud new dad: Shilton at home with wife Sue and new baby son Michael.

–LEGENDS–

Keith Weller

If Jimmy Bloomfield's genius was in bringing the best from brilliant but misunderstood individuals, then Keith Weller was as good an example as any of the great entertainers who charmed the Filbert Street fans in the 1970s.

A London lad whose career started but stalled at Spurs, his performances for Millwall convinced Chelsea to give him a chance but despite playing a role in their European Cup Winners' Cup triumph, he was never fully appreciated and Bloomfield paid £100,000 to prise him away from Stamford Bridge.

At Leicester he flourished, playing in midfield or attack with panache and flair, and just four England caps was a poor recognition of the range of his talent.

He was never afraid to be different or to try outlandish things – when they came off, as in his mazy run for the Goal of the Season in an FA Cup tie at Luton, they could be spectacular.

His temper sometimes got the better of him, as in the notorious incident when he refused to come out for the second half of a game against Ipswich, and knee injuries blighted the last few seasons of his time at City.

But nearly 300 games, almost all of them supplying a couple of moments of unique footballing magic, meant he could always be forgiven an occasional lapse.

He is perhaps best remembered nationally as the man who wore white tights for a freezing FA Cup tie, and that was just typical of an extravagant spirit that graced the club for eight magnificent years.

When he left Leicester City he moved to first play then manage in America, and it was a measure of how fondly he was remembered that when he later underwent a long, brave and ultimately fruitless fight against a rare form of cancer, the Leicester fans raised thousands of pounds to help him.

Keith Weller tussles with Liverpool's Kevin Keegan.

FOOTBALL
–STATS–

Keith Weller

Name: Keith Weller

Born: June 1946

Died: November 2004

Playing career: 1964–84

Clubs: Tottenham, Millwall, Chelsea, Leicester City, New England Tea Men, Fort Lauderdale Strikers, Fort Lauderdale Sun

Leicester appearances: 297

Goals: 43

England appearances: 4

Goals: 1

ABOVE: Ready for take-off! Some modern football stars hire private jets – Keith Weller started the trend by taking flying lessons.

LEFT & BELOW: White tights and red-hot football.

PAGE 26   DAILY MIRROR, Monday, January 8, 1979

FRANK McGHEE
Monday Verdict

BALLERINA WIELDING AN AXE..

Weller chops up a team that didn't try to play

Keith Weller, sporting a pair of white tights as the dancing master of Filbert Street.

Picture: DICK WILLIAMS

-LEGENDS-

Frank Worthington

In the 1960s George Best was considered the fifth Beatle. A decade later Frank Worthington was the second Elvis.

The king on the field, with extravagant skill and breathtaking ball-control, he was even more flamboyant off of it where he was one of the first to mix showbiz and sport.

It was the era when terms like "workrate" and "professionalism" had become the buzzwords of football, following the success of Don Revie's Leeds. Had Worthington run harder and faster he'd have won 100 England caps instead of just eight.

Instead he brought a laid-back brilliance to the field, exploding into life with wonderful flicks, touches or dribbles that thrilled crowds.

The new wave of coaches might have hated it, but Jimmy Bloomfield saw beyond that, and loved his flair and artistry. He bought him from Huddersfield, grabbing the chance to sign a star performer after a mooted move to Liverpool had fallen through.

He was the brightest star in a side of attacking thrills. It was a sign of Bloomfield's ability as a manager that he knew the way to get the best from him, and a sign of the change in football culture that successor Frank McLintock was happy to move him on to Bolton where he won the 1979 Golden Boot.

He spent the next 15 years as football's wandering minstrel, playing for a total of 24 clubs across the world, but more than 200 games while he was at Filbert Street means Leicester fans will always consider him to have been "their" special player.

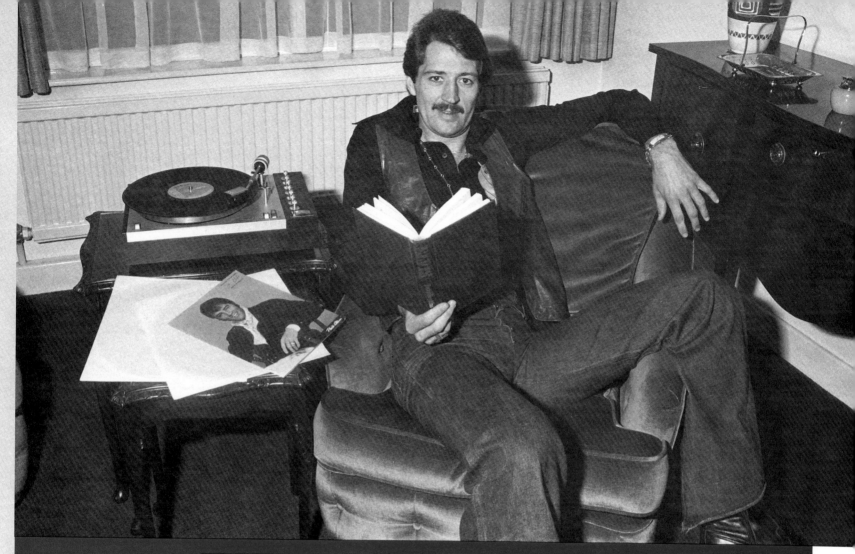

ABOVE: At home with his Elvis collection.

RIGHT: Worthington in action in a game against Tottenham at White Hart Lane.

141

Making the extraordinary look routine – Frank Worthington scores a spectacular diving header against Arsenal.

Scoring with a rocket shot against Liverpool in 1974.

LEFT:
England stars:
Worthington with
Peter Shilton.

FOOTBALL
–STATS–

Frank Worthington

Name: Frank Stewart Worthington

Born: November 1948

Playing career: 1966–92

Main clubs: Huddersfield, Leicester City, Bolton, Birmingham, Leeds, Sunderland, Southampton, Brighton, Tranmere, Preston, Stockport

Leicester appearances: 239

Goals: 78

England appearances: 8

Goals: 2

Keeping Cool

City players Steve Kember and Brian Anderson find ways to cool down during the heatwave in the summer of 1975.

–LEGENDS–

Mark Wallington

Still a teenager when he was bought from nearby Walsall to be Peter Shilton's understudy, the unspectacular but totally reliable Mark Wallington ended up playing more games for City than both Shilton and Gordon Banks.

Heavily influenced by Shilton's work ethic in training, he stepped into the first team in 1974 and was rarely out of it for the following nine seasons.

During that time he set a club record of 331 consecutive appearances, captained the club at one stage, and all this despite later revealing that he had suffered from a skin condition that at times stopped him training.

He was the solid rock behind the great entertainers team of the 1970s, remained loyal when Leicester were relegated at the end of the decade, and then played a significant and ever-present role in the side which regained top-flight status in 1983.

FOOTBALL –STATS–

Mark Wallington

Name: Francis Mark Wallington

Born: September 1952

Playing career: 1971–95

Clubs: Walsall, Leicester City, Derby, Lincoln, Grantham

Leicester appearances: 460

Goals: 78

England appearances: 8

–LEGENDS–

Steve Whitworth

Very much the prototype of a modern attacking full-back, Whitworth's pace and ability to time a tackle made him a superb defender – but it was his intelligence going forward that made him a perfect fit to support the flair players in front of him.

A product of Leicester's youth system, injuries gave him a chance in Frank O'Farrell's side that won promotion, but he then missed only three games in the entire six years of Jimmy Bloomfield's reign in the First Division.

Given his attacking instincts it was astonishing that he never registered a single competitive goal during his time at Filbert Street. It took him until the 570th game of his career, by which time he was at Mansfield, to put that right and even then it was by converting a penalty.

But the one time he did score for Leicester was at least important – it was the only goal of the 1971 FA Charity Shield success against Liverpool.

England manager Don Revie recognized his quality, giving him the chance to fill the right-back berth in 1975 and he won six more caps after his debut in a friendly against West Germany.

FOOTBALL –STATS–

Steve Whitworth

Name: Stephen Whitworth

Born: March 1952

Playing career: 1970–89

Clubs: Leicester City, Sunderland, Bolton, Mansfield, Barnet

Leicester appearances: 401

Goals: 1

England appearances: 7

Time for Change

Leicester's fans loved the excitement of Jimmy Bloomfield's flair players, but began to want something more tangible to show for it.

When the 1976–77 season started badly, Frank Worthington's comments – for which he was heavily fined – revealed some of the frustrations behind the scenes.

Being beaten 6-2 by Birmingham in December on a frozen Filbert Street pitch proved a turning point and though the side ultimately finished 11th in the First Division, within a week of the season ending the manager had resigned and Frank McLintock was on his way back to take over.

MANAGER McLINTOCK!

Frank says sad farewell—now for a top job

By KEVIN MOSELEY

FRANK McLINTOCK ended a distinguished playing career when Queen's Park Rangers drew 2—2 at home to Birmingham last night.

Afterwards, 37-year-old McLintock, commenting on speculation that he could take over the managership of Leicester, said: "I'm interested in any vacancy. I've always made it clear that I wanted to stay in the game when I retired. Beyond that, I'll just see what comes up."

McLintock was talking after Jimmy Bloomfield had resigned as Leicester manager. Immediately Bloomfield became favourite to take over Midlands rivals West Bromwich Albion.

Bloomfield receives around £40,000 because Leicester have paid up the remaining two years of a five-year contract. He remained loyal to the club last night, refusing to criticise.

"I'll let my record stand for itself," said 43-year-old Bloomfield, one of the shrewdest buyers and sellers in football. "I've given the club six years of my life and in return they've always been good to me. I haven't been as happy this season as I would have liked. I thought it was in the best interests of the club and myself to leave."

Boardroom interference, specially since the appointment of new director Colin McLeod, undoubtedly prompted Bloomfield's decision.

Back at QPR last night, Rangers and Birmingham players lined up to applaud skipper McLintock on to the field—and he took away a collection of silverware after several presentations.

McLintock said: "I'm an emotional man and I've been close to tears today."

Kick

You try to prepare yourself but it is still like a kick in the stomach when it finally comes."

Police battled to hold off hundreds of chanting fans who invaded the Loftus Road pitch after the final whistle and mobbed McLintock. The Scot was lost in the commotion and reappeared minutes later, minus his shirt.

Frank McLintock, minus his shirt, makes his emotional farewell at Queen's Park Rangers last night. Picture: BILL KENNEDY

'Worthy' fined and put on list

FRANK WORTHINGTON, Leicester's England striker, was put on the transfer list and fined a week's wages—probably £150—by the club yesterday.

The moves, both expected, followed criticisms he made of the team after Saturday's draw with Queen's Park Rangers.

"I didn't really know what expect, but the club have made the decision and it's up to me to accept it." Worthington said last night.

Derby, searching for a striker, could be interested

Signed

Leeds last night signed Burnley's 20-year-old England Under-23 striker Ray Hankin for £150,000, subject to the player passing a medical today.

Meanwhile, Leeds captain Billy Bremner has asked for more time to think over his proposed move to Second Division Hull

Aston Villa yesterday completed the £125,000 signing of Alex Cropley, 25, from Arsenal.

His Arsenal team-mate defender Terry Mancini, 33, has agreed terms with Aldershot, will sign a two-year contract for them today and make his debut in Saturday's home match with Swansea.

MONDAY VERDICT

Hat-trick star Burns lands a flash car..

Leicester a broken-down old banger

By DAVID MOORE: Leicester 2, Birmingham 6

BRAVERY as much as skill carried Birmingham to this six-hit success.

They were always ready to take the extra risk on a concrete-hard surface made doubly dangerous by its icy coating.

And the streamlined Soccer that earned a sleek sports car from a sponsor, when Kenny Burns headed goal No. 6 to complete his hat-trick, left Leicester looking like a broken-down banger.

Birmingham manager Willie Bell said afterwards: "I still believe the pitch was not fit for play, and I'm grateful that we have escaped without injury.

"It took real character to go out there and tackle the job like my lads did. I couldn't fault a single one of them—not that I want to."

Leicester boss Jimmy Bloomfield described his team's biggest home defeat for sixteen years as a "freak."

"Bravery must have played a part, although I can't say my players were lacking in that department," he said.

"Our biggest defenders couldn't tackle or turn and the conditions also prevented forwards who normally run with the ball from doing so properly.

"I don't deny that Birmingham deserved to win, but they are very much our bogy side, and there is always the chance that things will go badly against you on a pitch like this one."

"You simply can't apply the usual tactical considerations or criticisms in these circumstances."

The writing was always on the wall for Leicester, as Trevor Francis and Burns made a jet-propelled start, twisting and turning into space.

Chance

Burns held the ball beautifully before giving Gary Emmanuel the chance to score from 25 yards after 11 minutes.

Francis lashed in the second and Burns had headed two more before the break.

An own goal by Dennis Rofe and another strike by Burns completed the rout.

Leicester got scant consolation from late goals by Steve Kember and Frank Worthington, whose penalty took his tally to ten goals in 11 games.

We're killing the game—Worthy

FRANK WORTHINGTON used a condemnation of the way the English game is going as the basis for an astonishing post-match attack on his own team.

"A few more matches like that will kill the game," said the Leicester and England striker.

Worthington, a player who has always believed that entertaining is an essential part of Soccer, went on:

"If you thought it was bad today, you should have seen our match at Ipswich last week.

"We can't seem to string anything together. There's no build-up from

By HARRY MILLER

Leicester 2
QPR 2

the back. It's so frustrating for those of us up front.

"People are always telling me about the skill in our side. You tell me where it is."

Leicester have still to win a game this season. But what makes Worthington's view surprising is that six successive League draws also makes them one of only two unbeaten teams in the First Division.

Rangers were denied a victory they just about deserved by Chris Garland's last-minute header.

Before that, much of what we saw was indeed sub-standard.

A bad goalkeeping error by Phil Parkes allowed a mis-hit free kick by Dennis Rofe to give Leicester an early lead.

Don Givens equalised and a John Hollins shot helped by a deflection from Alan Woollett put Rangers ahead.

Rangers boss Dave Sexton was delighted with the impressive contribution of Stan Bowles and Don Givens.

PAGE 30   DAILY MIRROR, Monday, December 6, 1976

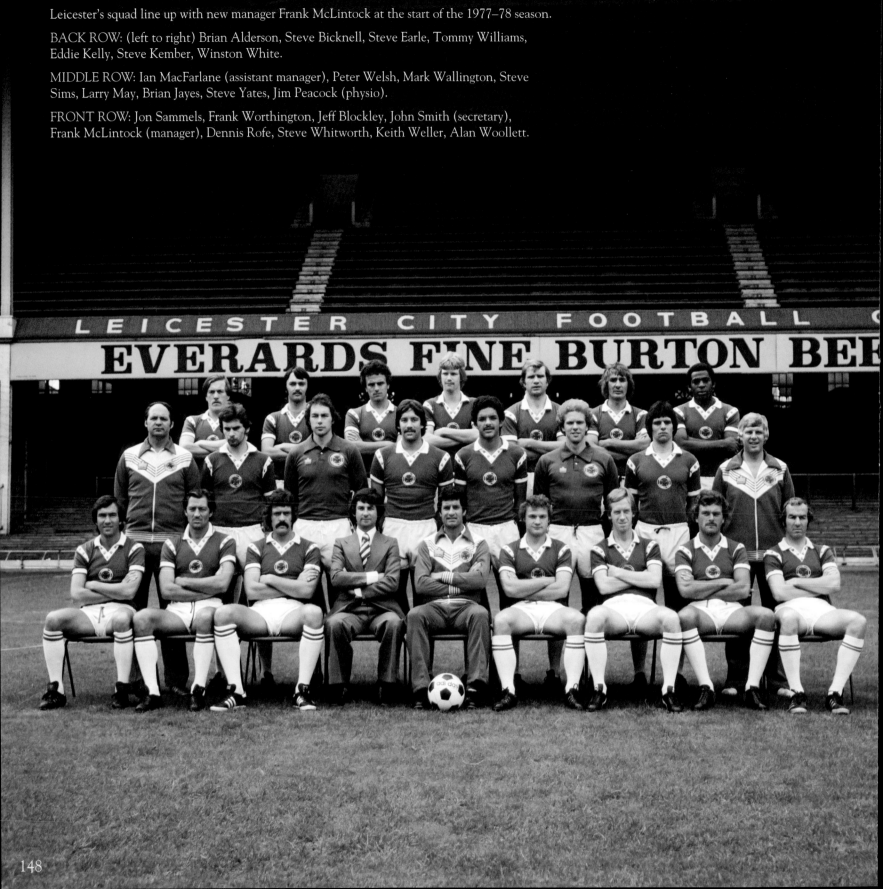

Leicester's squad line up with new manager Frank McLintock at the start of the 1977–78 season.

BACK ROW: (left to right) Brian Alderson, Steve Bicknell, Steve Earle, Tommy Williams, Eddie Kelly, Steve Kember, Winston White.

MIDDLE ROW: Ian MacFarlane (assistant manager), Peter Welsh, Mark Wallington, Steve Sims, Larry May, Brian Jayes, Steve Yates, Jim Peacock (physio).

FRONT ROW: Jon Sammels, Frank Worthington, Jeff Blockley, John Smith (secretary), Frank McLintock (manager), Dennis Rofe, Steve Whitworth, Keith Weller, Alan Woollett.

A Failed Experiment

McLintock was given a hero's welcome back to Leicester, with huge optimism about the potential of a new "tracksuit" manager.

Sadly he found there was more to the job than getting out on the training field, and his transfer dealings failed badly.

By the end of the season the once free-scoring Leicester had registered just 26 goals.

By April it was clear the experiment was over and McLintock resigned to return to his business interests in London before he was pushed.

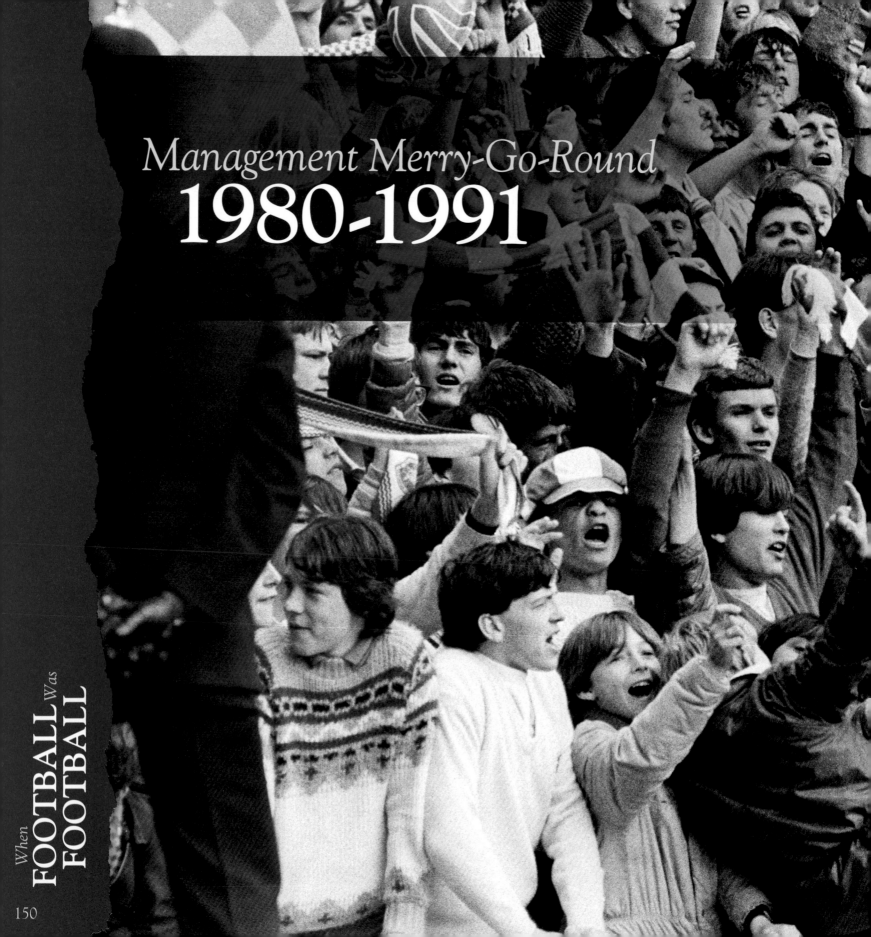

Management Merry-Go-Round
1980-1991

Excited Leicester fans celebrate promotion back to the First Division in 1983.

1980 Second Division title winners. **1981** Relegated; Gary Lineker's debut. **1982** FA Cup semi-final v Aston Villa; Jock Wallace resigns; Gordon Milne appointed. **1983** Promotion again after last-day drama and a Football League inquiry; Lineker wins the Second Division Golden Boot. **1984** Gary Lineker's first England cap. **1985** Lineker sold to Everton for £800,000. **1986** Bryan Hamilton is made joint manager with Milne. **1987** Relegation; Milne leaves and Hamilton takes over; Steve Walsh banned for 11 matches for breaking David Geddis' jaw; Hamilton sacked in December and replaced by David Pleat. **1989** Electronic scoreboard erected at Filbert Street. **1991** Pleat sacked; Gordon Lee is handed the caretaker role to the end of the season; City escape relegation to Division Three on last day; Brian Little appointed.

Leicester had stunned the football world in the summer of 1978 by going back to their Scottish traditions and capturing Jock Wallace from Glasgow giants Rangers.

His new broom swept through the club and brought change both on the field and behind the scenes. His commitment to a new youth policy included giving 18-year-old Gary Lineker his debut, and he also gave the side a new discipline and better fitness.

By the end of his second season it had paid dividends as his side swept to the Second Division Championship.

LEFT: Jock Wallace celebrates promotion as Leicester's fans flood the Filbert Street pitch.

BELOW: Liverpool legend and four-times Manager of the Year Bob Paisley presents Wallace with a special award to recognize his achievement.

Near Miss

Excited Leicester fans greet their team from the Holte End at Villa Park.

HARRY MILLER hands the honours to Hoddle

THE IRONY was not lost on Leicester's players.

Outside, the vociferous horde of celebrating Tottenham fans were still chanting "There's only one Ardiles."

Inside, in the sad sanctuary of a dressing room where beaten FA Cup semi-finalists go to lick their wounds, the talk was of another Tottenham player – Glenn Hoddle.

For ninety intriguing minutes, Ardiles – for reasons far divorced from football – had been the target for massive support on our side and muddled abuse on the other.

Hoddle knew that he, more than any other, could take some of the immense pressure off the departing Argentinian.

He did it with a performance that was scintillating even by his own recent sky-high standards.

Vision

Hoddle stood up to Leicester's expected early aggression, then took control to mastermind what became a comprehensive Tottenham victory.

Later, it was almost as if Leicester manager Jock Wallace was his most experienced player. Eddie Kelly, were competing for president of the Midlands branch of Hoddle's fan club.

"The lad was an absolute revelation – especially to my players," said Wallace.

"If we are going to achieve anything at all, it is Hoddle's sort of vision and passing ability we have got to try to emulate.

"He is a superb player, a complete player."

Kelly spoke for the rest of Leicester's dejected Second Division side when he said: "The lads are all asking whether Hoddle is human or not.

"When I was with Arsenal, I played for a while with Liam Brady. I always thought he was the most muddled player around. I was wrong.

"He should be an abso-

THE COMPLETE KIND OF PLAYER

Spurs 2, Leicester 0

lutely automatic choice whenever an England side is named.

Hoddle's acceptance that Ardiles might be a few degrees under, his determination to do that bit more, confirmed the consistency that is now a welcome part of his game.

Spurs manager Keith Burkinshaw pinpointed the difference between the Hoddle of now and two years ago when he said: "Glenn has become a responsible team member – it is the team that matters most to him."

On the day Hoddle shone and Ardiles showed what being a good professional is all about, Tottenham had others to thank for reaching their second successive FA Cup final.

Skipper Steve Perryman and Graham Roberts were sound and uncompromising in a defence that experienced few anxious moments, while Mike Hazard emphasised he is surely at the point where Tottenham would find it impossible to leave him out.

Leicester, for 45 minutes, did the something as they had promised and we all expected.

Andy Peake and veteran Kelly could be proud of the part they played. In fact, it was only delayed the inevitable.

Alan Young, injured in the first half, had just been replaced by Jim

Melrose when Spurs scored in the 55th minute.

Hoddle's short corner was played across goal by Ardiles and Garth Crooks beat keeper Mark Wallington with a ferocious volley.

Tottenham's second goal was a personal heartbreak for Ian Wilson. He put the ball into his own net after 77 minutes with a delicate lob of which master craftsman Hoddle himself would have been proud.

Roberts limped off before the end with a groin strain. But he expects to be fit to face Barcelona in the Cup Winners Cup on Wednesday.

GOTCHA! Leicester's John O'Neill gets shirty with Steve Archibald.

GOTCHA! Crooks consoles own-goal Wilson.

GOTCHA! Glenn Hoddle puts the 'scissors' on high-flying O'Neill.   *Pictures: MONTE FRESCO*

Nobody could accuse Wallace of lacking ambition in the First Division – he even tried and failed to sign Dutch legend Johan Cruyff.

But the reality failed to match his lofty ideas and City slipped back into the Second Division. It meant another attempt to rebuild, but a poor start to the season meant Wallace's team, in which Gary Lineker was maturing rapidly after establishing himself as first-choice number nine, had too much to do to get back into the promotion race.

There was, however, the consolation of an FA Cup run and wins over Southampton, Hereford, Watford and Shrewsbury which earned a day out at Villa Park for a semi-final with Tottenham.

The defeat proved to be Wallace's last big day – at the end of the season he accepted an offer to return to Scotland and manage Motherwell.

LEFT: How the *Mirror* reported Glenn Hoddle's virtuoso display for Spurs.

BELOW: Match action from the semi-final.

Confusion

New manager Gordon Milne reshuffled the side but results took time to materialize. A crowd of just 6,155, the lowest home gate since the Second World War, saw City play Shrewsbury in mid-February.

That turned out to be the start of a 15-match unbeaten run, but there was drama to come before Leicester's promotion could be confirmed.

A 0-0 draw at home to already-relegated Burnley left them needing Fulham to lose at Derby. The final whistle blew at the Baseball Ground on a 1-0 home win, only for the referee to reveal he had blown more than a minute early because of crowd trouble.

It left the Football League having to sort out the mess, and an anxious wait before the result stood.

LEFT & RIGHT: An anxious Gordon Milne waits for news from the Baseball Ground to find out if his side are really going up.

A Promotion Party

Both players and fans didn't care about events at Derby – they believed they had won promotion fair and square and the celebrations followed.

Instead it took another four days before a four-hour Football League inquiry ruled in their favour.

–LEGENDS–

Gary Lineker

Arguably the most instinctive finisher of the modern era and the man who failed only by one missed penalty to match Sir Bobby Charlton's record for most England goals, began his football life as an eager-eyed Leicester teenager.

Ironically there were doubts about his potential at first. His blistering turn of pace meant he was used mainly as a winger, until Gordon Milne harnessed him in a three-pronged attack with Alan Smith and Steve Lynex.

The winner of the Golden Boot in the Second Division during the promotion campaign of 1983, he was then second only to Ian Rush for most goals in the top flight the next year, and a further 12 months down the line he was joint top scorer with Chelsea's Kerry Dixon on 24.

When Bobby Robson picked out this emerging talent to bring him into the England squad ahead of the 1986 World Cup, it was inevitable that Leicester would not be able to hold him much longer, and they accepted an £800,000 bid in 1985 from League champions Everton.

Gary Lineker (centre) celebrates his 1983 Second Division Golden Boot with Scunthorpe's Steve Cammock (left) and Reading's Kerry Dixon – top scorers in the Fourth and Third Divisions respectively.

BOBBY'S YOUNG BEAUTS

By FRANK McGHEE

England 2, Rep. of Ireland 1

ENGLAND reaped a rich reward despite having two key players injured at Wembley last night.

While skipper Bryan Robson and Mark Hateley fell to reckless Irish fouls, England had the considerable consolation of so many eager World Cup hopefuls performing so brightly.

The verdict on almost all those who were either totally untried or whose international careers can be measured in minutes rather than matches, has to be one of enthusiastic approval.

The solitary sad exception was goalkeeper Gary Bailey. He had only one real save to make, two minutes from time—and made a mess of it, allowing a shot from Liam Brady to squirm out of his grasp and under his body—to make the result sound like a reasonable contest.

It wasn't—and the less familiar faces in the England team can all glow with pride.

New cap Chris Waddle lived up to the promise he has shown for Newcastle, full of confidence and intricate skills.

Trevor Steven and Gary Lineker, each with only one previous appearance, scored lovely goals and the second of these was laid on by another new boy Peter Davenport.

Expertise

They would all, however, be happy to concede the debts they owed to the quality of the support they received from more famous names.

Kenny Sansom had a superb game, quick and intelligent. Ray Wilkins, revelling in the return of Robson, had all his old accuracy and expertise flooding back. It has to be conceded, of course, that individually the Irish could not hope to match the depth of England's quality.

Only two Irishmen presented England with anything like the problems they can expect in world-class encounters to come. Mark Lawrenson was a superb marshal of a defence that held out for

ABOVE: How the *Mirror* reported Lineker's full England debut.

BELOW: Lineker celebrating a goal against Manchester United at Filbert Street in 1984.

Lineker shows his instinct for goal by going round Stoke goalkeeper Barry Siddall in a game at Filbert Street.

FOOTBALL
-STATS-

Gary Lineker

Name: Gary Winston Lineker

Born: November 1960

Playing career: 1978–94

Clubs: Leicester City, Everton, Barcelona, Tottenham, Nagoya Grampus Eight

Leicester appearances: 216

Goals: 103

England appearances: 80

Goals: 48

ABOVE: Moving on: Lineker with Everton manager Howard Kendall after an £800,000 transfer fee had been fixed by tribunal.

BELOW: Gordon Milne had big plans to use the cash.

GARY'S PRICE IS RIGHT

GARY LINEKER'S £800,000 transfer fee for joining League champions Everton will make Leicester a better team.

That was last night's pledge from Leicester boss Gordon Milne, after a League tribunal fixed the figure following 90 minutes of hard bargaining at FA headquarters in London.

Milne, who reckons Lineker's goals saved Leicester from relegation last season, promised: "I will use the cash to buy three players, reinforcing Leicester's side all round.

"Everton have gained a superb performer for their money," added Milne, now chasing a list of transfer targets including Dundee United star forward Paul Sturrock and Liverpool's ex-Leicester midfield player Kevin McDonald.

–LEGENDS–

Alan Smith

If you've ever put your last coin in the slot machine, walked away and then watched the next player hit the jackpot, you'd know exactly how Jock Wallace would feel about Alan Smith.

The last transfer deal the Scot did before facing up to his failure to restore City to the First Division was to sign the gangly centre-forward from non-League Alvechurch, because he'd liked what he'd seen of the part-timer in the Southern League.

One of the first things his successor Gordon Milne then did was to pair Smith in an attacking formation with talented young striker Gary Lineker.

For next to nothing he'd got a pair which ultimately brought in £1.6 million in transfer fees to the Filbert Street coffers – but contributed goals by the bucketload in the meantime.

They were the ideal partnership – Smith with his height and willing work rate created chances for Lineker with his instinctive finishing ability.

Smith was also a loyal club man. He stayed two more seasons after Lineker's move to Everton, taking on his own shoulders more of the burden of getting goals, and then once his move to Arsenal had been agreed negotiated a loan back to Leicester to do his best in what proved ultimately a lost fight against relegation.

RIGHT: Beating Liverpool's Mark Lawrenson to the ball.

FOOTBALL
–STATS–
Alan Smith

Name: Alan Martin Smith

Born: November 1962

Playing career: 1981–95

Clubs: Alvechurch, Leicester City, Arsenal

Leicester appearances: 217

Goals: 84

England appearances: 13

Goals: 2

ABOVE: Deadly duo: Gary Lineker tries a shot as Alan Smith starts running to look for any rebound.

BELOW: In action against Liverpool at Filbert Street.

Revolving Door

Milne's optimistic belief that he could make Leicester stronger after selling Gary Lineker proved unfounded.

His team stayed up by one point thanks to a final-day win over Newcastle in 1986, and the directors voted to bring in Bryan Hamilton as joint boss.

That proved a disaster. City were relegated in 1987 and Milne left to leave the Northern Ireland international in sole charge.

By December the winds of change were blowing again. Hamilton went with the team in 16th place and former Tottenham boss David Pleat was installed.

Pleat led them to finish 13th, 15th and 13th again, and Leicester were in the Second Division relegation zone when he too was sacked in January 1991. Gordon Lee became the next in the manager's office, and an edgy 1-0 win over Oxford on the last day eked out Leicester's survival.

But it was time for change once more, and in the summer of 1991 Brian Little was summoned to the rescue.

Bad Days

It was a bleak period in Leicester's history and the constant struggles were summed up on the final day of the 1989–90 season when Sheffield United arrived needing a win to avoid relegation.

Leicester gave a dismal display – made worse when goalkeeper Martin Hodge had to go off injured and centre-half Marc North was handed the gloves.

United's fans had a double celebration that day. They watched their team dish out a 5-2 hammering to secure their own survival – and then heard news that bitter rivals Wednesday had been relegated from Division One.

Little by Little
1992-1995

Life in the fast lane – motorcycle fan Brian Little put
Leicester on the road to success.

1992 Wembley play-off defeat to Blackburn. **1993** Another Wembley play-off defeat, this time to Swindon; new main stand built at Filbert Street. **1994** Third time lucky beating Derby in Wembley play-off final to reach Premier League. **1995** Brian Little walks out to join Aston Villa; Mark McGhee appointed; Leicester are relegated.

Close . . .

Brian Little, once an Aston Villa star whose career was cruelly cut short by injury, was actually the second choice of chairman Martin George to take over from David Pleat.

He'd forged a reputation in management working on a shoestring by earning two promotions in two years at Darlington and brought the same buoyant confidence to Filbert Street.

A flying start gave way to an inconsistent campaign, but then a storming 5-0 second-leg win over Cambridge set up Leicester's first outing to Wembley for 25 years.

The day ended in disappointment. A Steve Walsh challenge sent David Speedie stumbling and Mike Newell scored the resulting penalty which settled the game.

RIGHT: The dejected Leicester players after the final whistle against Blackburn.

Closer . . .

A year later and Brian Little's team were back at Wembley for another play-off final, this time as huge favourites against Swindon.

  Just when everything seemed to be going wrong, with City 3-0 down after half-time, along came an ecstatic 12 minutes as goals by Julian Joachim, Steve Walsh and Steve Thompson brought the game level . . .

Leicester players – and fans – enjoy the celebrations during a dramatic Wembley goal spree.

. . . *But Still So Far Away*

Who could believe that just 12 months after Leicester fans felt robbed by a penalty decision at Wembley, yet another big refereeing call would go against them?

With six minutes of normal time remaining, referee David Elleray adjudged that goalkeeper Kevin Poole had brought down Steve White, and Paul Bodin calmly put away the winner.

At the end there was dejection – and the determination from Brian Little to get it right next time.

Hero . . . and Villain

It was to be another season of inconsistency. Little's team hit top spot in January in what was now called – since the creation of the Premier League – the Endsleigh League Division One. But results tailed away again, and angry fans turned on the manager after a dismal 1-1 draw in April.

A few weeks later they were hailing him as a semi-final win over Tranmere brought another trip to Wembley, and this time it was destined to end in victory.

Steve Walsh's two goals beat neighbours Derby, and Simon Grayson became the first Leicester captain ever to climb the Wembley stairs to collect a trophy.

Gaining promotion was one thing – staying there another. By November Little's team had won just two matches, and when his old club Aston Villa came knocking to offer him the chance to return as manager he caused more fury by walking out – a point made clear to him when one of his first games in charge of his new club was back at Filbert Street.

DAILY MIRROR, Tuesday, May 31, 1994   PAGE 23

Steve puts Leicester back in the big time

PREM-GLEE!

Walsh's joy day

Derby 1 Leicester 2

By TONY STENSON

THERE were unashamed tears as Leicester finally beat their Wembley jinx yesterday and returned to the big stage.

Two goals from Steve Walsh — so much forgotten because of injury that he didn't rate a mention in the programme — started a night of street parties in Leicester to celebrate the end of their seven-year absence from life in the fast lane.

Leicester's dramatic First Division play-off victory proved money can't guarantee success.

Bristling

Derby's £12 million spending spree has again failed to buy promotion, and that leaves manager Roy McFarland's future hanging by a thread. Their millionaire owner Lionel Pickering made it clear Big Mac's job hung on the result of this Wembley shoot-out.

Not that it concerned Leicester. They had previously made six Wembley visits, only to be left at the altar every time.

Derby, bristling with more individual skill, had taken an early lead through Tommy Johnson and should have had it bagged and posted by the time Leicester decided to stop clogging and start playing.

Walsh, written off last August with a severed cruciate ligament, launched their recovery

HE'S DONE IT: Goal hero Steve Walsh is congratulated after his equaliser   Picture: BRENDAN MONKS

and then snatched a dramatic winner three minutes from the end.

Paul Simpson split Leicester's defence with a raking, 50-yard pass that Johnson controlled, shrugging off Simon Grayson's challenge to turn the ball into the net after 26 minutes.

It was a false dawn. The game was blown wide open when Walsh rose above Derby's defence to head that Grayson intercepted and crossed for Ian Ormondroyd to thunderously head at Derby keeper Gavin Ward.

Control

It seemed to work as they pegged back the most expensive team assembled outside the Premier League.

Derby, however, eventually managed to control the pace of the game and took the lead using the long ball themselves.

But you would still have put your money on Derby to snatch victory until Joachim arrived to spice and speed Leicester's attack.

Delight

Two telling runs paved the way for a glorious pass inside the full-back that Grayson intercepted and crossed for Ian Ormondroyd to thunderously head at Derby keeper Gavin Ward.

The drama wasn't over. Ward palmed brilliantly

missed, and the ball bounced over his shoulder into the net.

Walsh punched the air in sheer delight to end his own personal journey of drama.

He was converted from centre-half to striker and stripped of the club captaincy by manager Brian Little because he kept being sent off.

He scored regularly until his painful and career-threatening injury.

Little gambled on bringing him back early and the move suited everyone — except Roy McFarland

out, only for Walsh to toe back into the net with just three minutes remaining.

MIRROR DERBY **4 PAGE RACE SPECIAL**

DON'T MISS IT TOMORROW!

PLUS TODAY YOUR SUPER DERBY SWEEP KIT

STEVIE WONDER LEICESTER'S double diamond Steve Walsh turns away to celebrate his winning goal that sent Brian Little's side into the Premiership.

TEAR-IFIC!

CRYING GAME DERBY'S Wembley defeat leaves striker Tommy Johnson in tears – and in need of comfort from team-mate Paul Williams

By HUGH JAMIESON
Leicester 2, Derby 1

JUBILANT Leicester yesterday buried a Wembley jinx — and left manager Brian Little in tears of joy.

Leicester bridged a seven-year gap to grab a dream £2.5million Premiership ticket to the big time, thanks to a dramatic winner from comeback star Steve Walsh three minutes from time.

Leicester's players celebrated in style as the club finally ended a Wembley nightmare of six defeats spanning 45 years.

They had lost four FA Cup finals and then endured the horror of two successive First Division play-off final defeats at the hands of Blackburn and Swindon.

Little, in tears at the end, admitting: "We tried so hard about it being third time lucky, although so many people had told us it was going to be our year.

"Now it's turned out that way and obviously it's a marvellous feeling, especially after so much bitter disappointment involving the last two play-off finals."

Little hailed Walsh after his goal rush killed off Derby. He said: "He's different class."

Walsh played only his second full game in seven months after being written off for the season with damaged cruciate knee ligaments.

Little added: "Everyone knows Steve has had his problems in the past with discipline because of his short fuse.

"But when fit he's the first name on the team sheet and I don't think Leicester could afford to go out and buy someone like him.
PREM-GLEE – Page 23

Mirror SCORE

I'M OFF! Little leaving yesterday

Little's 3-way winner

By DAVID MOORE

● POKER-faced boss Brian Little could pat himself on the back last night for pulling the three-card trick after walking out on Leicester City.

● With bottom-of-the-table Leicester still shell-shocked before this evening's home game against Arsenal, Little is now all set to move in as Aston Villa's new £250,000-a-year manager.

● No wonder Filbert Street chairman Martin George was left sweating buckets, perhaps fearing for his own job, following a dramatic board meeting at which Little coolly took Leicester to the cleaners!

● Firstly, millionaire George, a member of the 'Weetabix' family, and six fellow directors meekly accepted Little's resignation. They even offered 'sincere thanks for his immense contribution.'

● Secondly, Little is also totally free to decide his own future, which is bound to include early talks with Villa supremo Doug Ellis. "We can't block any approach from here on," admitted the tight-lipped George.

● Thirdly, despite Leicester's threat to demand a staggering £1.5m for losing Little, Ellis suddenly doesn't need to pay a single penny in compensation to land his No1 target.

● So it looks like former Villa and England striker Little has beaten the clock, if he and Ellis are racing to shake hands on a deal, as most people suspect.

● Little – spat on by Leicester fans in April – insisted: "My conscience is clear. I utterly deny speaking to Villa already."

Ilie stuck on the sideline

● ILIE Dumitrescu looks certain to be left out by new boss Gerry Francis amid fears for his Spurs future.

● The World Cup ace is resigned to sitting out the home clash with Chelsea despite completing a one-match ban. Dumitrescu said: "My suspension is over but I was even told on Monday I wasn't playing.

● Francis said: "We have a number of gifted players, I cannot accommodate them all."

Big man Little

By HUGH JAMIESON

LITTLE AND LARGE: Striker Ian Ormondroyd dwarfs his boss

BRIAN LITTLE, the man spat on this season by Leicester fans, could today be a Wembley hero.

Little leads Leicester into a third successive First Division play off final against Midlands rivals Derby admitting: "It was the worst moment of my career."

He suddenly found himself under fire during Leicester's 1-1 draw at home to Grimsby last month as a group of fans jeered and spat at him as he walked up the tunnel at half-time.

Little said: "I've been taught over 25 years in the game as a player and manager how to handle certain situations.

"On this occasion I had to count to 10 before walking away because if I'd stayed there I could have been involved in an argument or had a fight that would have served no purpose.

Beaten

"We had 10 players out injured at the time and were beaten twice in successive games at home.

"It was my first experience of something like that and I certainly didn't enjoy it, so I stayed away from the touchline in the second half and watched the rest of the game from an executive box.

"At the time, I suppose the fans must have thought promotion was slipping away and their frustration boiled over, but there was no excuse for that kind of hooliganism."

As Little aims for a £3 million premiership ticket, Leicester chairman Martin George said: "He's a class act.

"That ugly situation could have been the turning point of our season, because 95 per cent of the fans rallied round afterwards.

"Everyone had been watching him to see how he would react and he was brilliant, just as he has been in three years at Filbert Street.

"Everybody is in place at the club and after two years of bitter disappointment we're all hoping it's third time lucky."

Little now faces his toughest decision of the season with 13-goal Welsh star Iwan Roberts, midfield man Steve Agnew and defender Colin Hill all chasing the chance of a recall

MARTIN'S MAGIC

By ROGER WARE: Wycombe 4, Preston 2

WYCOMBE set themselves up as the "next Wimbledon" with a Wembley super show which catapulted them into the Second Division at their first attempt.

But there are subtle differences between the Dons and Wycombe – notably that Martin O'Neill's happy Wanderers play high quality passing football, have a rather more gentlemanly approach, and have their own smart new stadium.

O'Neill's men were twice behind in this Third Division play-off final. Ian Bryson put Preston ahead, but Steve Thompson equalised. Paul Raynor grabbed a second for Preston. Then a Simon Garner goal and two from Dave Carroll wrapped it up for Wycombe in the second-half.

You're a coward, Doug!

LITTLE SUPPORT
NEW Villa boss Brian Little is left to face the flak on his own at Filbert Street as chairman Doug Ellis didn't attend

George blasts no-show Ellis

ASTON VILLA chairman Doug Ellis was labelled "the Coward of the County" last night, after failing to turn up on Brian Little's day of hate!

While new Villa boss Little was left to face the music, following his controversial walk-out on Leicester, Deadly Doug was nowhere to be found.

And counterpart Martin George, poised to step up City's fight for £500,000 compensation over losing Little, had no hesitation in aiming the cruel jibe in the direction of Ellis.

George said: "If Ellis had come to this match and walked into our Boardroom, I'd have cracked open a bottle of best champagne — over his head!"

Poaching

"Nobody needs to find excuses for why Mr. Ellis wasn't here. The reasons are blindingly obvious.

"I've heard the remark about the coward of the county, and I agree with it. Aston Villa and Doug Ellis owe us for poaching Brian Little's services. Everybody in football knows what went on, and we shan't rest until we obtain satisfaction."

Little, appointed as Ron Atkinson's £200,000-a-year successor, looked surprised when he said: "I didn't know my chairman wasn't here.

"It was possibly the worst day of my life. Being called a liar and a Judas isn't very nice.

Yesterday, Little revealed: "I was just glad to get out of the place in one

By DAVID MOORE: Leicester 1, Aston Villa 1

piece, after slogging my guts out for Leicester for more than three years, I thought I deserved better."

But millionaire George scoffed: "What on earth did Brian expect? He left us in the lurch."

Attack

Sacked Villa boss Atkinson also went on the attack against Ellis.

Big Ron spoke of his anger at being fired, accusing Ellis of "a major gaffe" — and also claiming he'd have won Villa a trophy this season.

Ellis gave Atkinson the boot after Villa went nine Premiership games without a win.

But Atkinson, speaking on Danny Baker's TV chat show, said: "I feel angry and disappointed. We've had three great years at Villa, and the team is a good side.

"Ok, they dipped, but just five weeks ago people were saying they'd given the best display by an English side for years against Inter Milan."

A fans' poll showed 87 per cent wanted Atko reinstated. He said: "I would have gone back."

While Little was close to breaking point off the pitch, on the field it was Leicester who nearly crumbled in a scrappy relegation fight.

FANS FOR NOTHING: Leicester supporters display their fury over Little's departure to Villa

---

Roger and out

Southend 2, Swindon 0

SOUTHEND midfielder Roger Willis had five stitches in his gashed nose and X-rays in hospital after the ugly clash that earned Steve McMahon a red card on his debut as Swindon player-boss.

McMahon claimed it was an accidental collision. "There's no way I deliberately elbowed him," he said.

Southend boss Peter Taylor said: "Willis is in a pretty bad way – he didn't know where he was when we got him back to the dressing room. Whatever happened it was a nasty injury."

Referee Steve Gunn said: "I sent McMahon off for violent conduct."

McMahon had earlier been booked for a bruising challenge on Phil Gridelet but for the most part he had to watch his former Liverpool pal Ronnie Whelan totally dominate the midfield.

Whelan's second minute free kick led to Willis heading Southend in front. Swindon keeper Fraser Digby presented Andy Edwards with No2.

❝It was possibly the worst day of my life❞

In Brian Little's place came Mark McGhee, the former Aberdeen player with a reputation gained as manager of Reading for playing fluent, attractive football.

He couldn't halt the slide back to the second tier, but when the next season began with a Manager of the Month award, and City top of the table, there were high hopes.

Instead it ended in anger and acrimony as in December struggling Wolves came knocking on his door and McGhee chose to take the offer.

For the second time in a year a manager had walked out on Leicester, and there was fury among the fans while a bitter feud developed between the clubs before a compensation payment was finally agreed.

McGhee stunner

By DAVID MOORE

MARK McGHEE is being offered a mind-bending £500,000 a year to walk out on Leicester and become manager of Wolves.

That's the bonanza, including a bonus for winning promotion, that McGhee, 38, can bank by waving goodbye to Filbert Street.

The Molineux offer will rocket McGhee to the top of British soccer's managerial pay league – and it explains why he is ready to rip up the remaining 18 months of his Leicester contract.

It would put McGhee on double the figure his close friend Alex Ferguson earns from Manchester United, as a basic salary.

McGhee, planning to take assistant Colin Lee and coach Mike Hickman with him to Wolves, said yesterday: "I'm prepared to face the flak which will be thrown at me. But I can leave with a clear conscience."

Wolves snare Mark but at a high price

MARK McGHEE finally became a happy Wanderer last night by declaring: "Wolves can fulfil my every ambition."

The 38-year-old Scot became one of Britain's highest-paid managers after signing a three-and-a-half year deal reckoned to be worth £1.5million. And then he claimed: "I believe I would now remain at Wolves even if a big club like Rangers, Newcastle or even Manchester United came in for me."

McGhee was installed as new Molineux boss after more than 10 days of wrangling between Wolves and Leicester, which eventually brought the latter around £1m in compensation.

The O'Neill Era
1996-2000

A winner. Martin O'Neill celebrates the first of three League Cup triumphs after a dramatic extra-time success against Middlesbrough.

1996 Martin O'Neill starts with one win in 11 games – then wins promotion at Wembley v Crystal Palace. **1997** League Cup final victory over Middlesbrough after a replay; UEFA Cup run ends v Atlético Madrid; Leicester is listed on the Alternative Investment Market. **1998** Plans for a new stadium unveiled; O'Neill turns down approach to take over Leeds United. **1999** League Cup final v Tottenham. **2000** Another League Cup final triumph, this time v Tranmere; Emile Heskey sold to Liverpool for club record £11 million; O'Neill leaves to become manager of Celtic.

MIRROR SPORT • MIRROR SPORT • MIRROR SPORT

2 SECS QUICKIE BRINGS DOWN PALACE

C Palace 1 Leicester 2 (aet)

By TONY STENSON

SHATTERED Crystal Palace's Premiership dream died TWO seconds from a Wembley penalty shoot-out yesterday.

That's how long was left on the referee's watch when Leicester's Steve Claridge scored the wonder goal that broke Dave Bassett's heart and sent Leicester into the big-time.

The play-off was 40 seconds into extra-time injury time when Claridge's goal stunned Palace fans into silence.

Bassett choked back the tears and said: "It's the third time I've had sand kicked in my face after being so close to something.

"I must have killed a few robins in my life because no one deserves this." But he put on a brave face to joke: "As they say: 'When you win you can smile, when you lose you can please your f****** self'."

It was a miracle for Bassett even to get to Wembley. Palace were 15th when he took over in February, but he launched an amazing 22-game run, losing only four.

Bassett added: "It doesn't count for anything now."

CRYST-HELL PALACE – Pages 32, 33

BASSETT: Choked

★ AGONY AND ECSTASY: Palace's George Ndah (right) can't believe what has happened as Leicester celebrate their last-gasp win

HAIR LOSS?

New manager Martin O'Neill's reign started badly with just one win – ironically away to Mark McGhee's Wolves – in his first 11 League matches.

But a couple of key signings began to make a difference – most notably a flame-haired midfielder from humble Crewe by the name of Neil Lennon, and striker Steve Claridge from Birmingham.

When he then added another midfield man, Muzzy Izzet, on loan from Chelsea's reserves, it sparked a run of six wins and a draw from the final eight matches – and an unexpected place in the play-off places.

That meant another outing to Wembley and high drama as Claridge's goal in virtually the final minute of extra-time meant Leicester were back in the Premier League.

WEMBLEY SPECIAL WEMBLEY SPECIAL WEMBLEY SPECIAL WEMBLEY SPECIAL WEMBL

IT'S CRYST-HELL PALACE!

HIGH HOPES: Joy as Andy Roberts puts Palace into an early lead

Last-gasp agony for Bassett

By TONY STENSON

SUDDENLY, Dave Bassett ran out of miracles. And it left Leicester celebrating a return to the Premiership a year after disappearing through the relegation trap door.

Palace manager Bassett, soccer's magic man, suffered a spear-thrust to the heart as Palace suffered the cruellest of play-off cuts.

The game was 40 seconds into extra-time injury-time and just two seconds from a penalty shoot-out when Leicester's Steve Claridge mis-hit a shot from 20 yards.

The ball wrong-footed Palace keeper Nigel Martyn and went in.

Bankrupt gambler Claridge, who admits he has lost £250,000 to the bookies, had finally hit the jackpot.

Sand

Bassett said: "It's the third time I've had sand kicked in my face after being so close to something.

"I must have killed a few robins in my life because, surely, no one deserves this.

"The boys battled but didn't use the ball well. The Wembley occasion got to some of them.

"You can say we're upset after being 15 minutes from promotion when losing at Derby and then having to fight a play-off after finishing third. But we knew the rules.

"Now I'll sit down with our chairman Ron Noades and decide where the future lies."

Palace were in 15th place when Bassett took over in February. But he launched an amazing 22-game run, losing only four to get in sight of Wembley.

Defeat will cost Palace £4million

Crystal Palace 1 Leicester 2

THE PARTY'S OVER: The misery of defeat hits Bruce Dyer (left) and George Ndah at Wembley

in lost revenue — but it all started so well when they went ahead after 13 minutes.

Ray Houghton and David Hopkin combined to put Andy Roberts clear to smash in from 18 yards.

Then Leicester took over, until they finally became an unstoppable steam-roller.

Palace defender Marc Edworthy cracked and brought down Muzzy Izzet from Colin Walsh's raking

pass. Garry Parker rifled home the 76th minute penalty.

Then it was all Leicester until Claridge finally made the break through.

Leicester manager Martin O'Neill had sent on 6ft 7ins substitute keeper Zeljko Kalac, hoping his height would be an advantage in the penalty shoot-out.

The giant Aussie had just made the goal-line when Julian Watts

headed down and Claridge rifled home.

"I did mis-hit it, but what the hell! It went in — that's all that matters. It just sat up and I was amazed no one went for it," he said.

O'Neill enjoyed the moment. He started his Leicester run with Norwich fans accusing him of walking out on them to take over at Filbert Street.

And after nine games without a victory he admitted: "I did begin to worry. It was the lowest point of my career.

"But we thoroughly deserved it — and what's more, we will stay up this time!"

Referee David Allison said: "As the ball hit the net I looked at my watch and there were two seconds left."

ROYLE CHASES £4M DEAN

JOE ROYLE is poised to follow up his £3.5million swoop for Gary Speed with a renewed £4m bid for Dean Holdsworth.

The Everton boss wants a 20-goal-a-season partner for Duncan Ferguson and the Wimbledon striker has been a long-term target.

But Royle needs a summer clear-out to help balance the books. Anders Limpar and Daniel Amokachi are top of the exit list.

Mac to axe absent Roy

By CATHAL DERVAN

ROY Keane phoned home last night but Mick McCarthy wasn't available to take the call.

The missing Manchester United star, back in England after a holiday in Capri, rang the Dublin Airport hotel to make his peace with Ireland boss McCarthy.

But as Keane made the call McCarthy was getting to grips with the FAI golf classic at Luttrellstown.

As he arrived at last night's Irish soccer writers' banquet in Dublin, McCarthy said: "Unfortunately I wasn't there to take the call. I can only hope that since Roy made contact once, he will try to make contact again.

"I would still like to speak to him. As I said already, I would have liked a bit explaining where he was. Maybe he's done that much now."

Even if Keane arrives in Dublin this evening, he will not captain the Republic against Portugal tomorrow night. And McCarthy added: "It's looking highly unlikely that they will play."

KEANE: Phone call

Ruud's cash splash

MANAGER Ruud Gullit is facing the first big test of his Chelsea transfer market plans after his £4.5million capture of Gianluca Vialli.

Gullit wants to land at least one more big-money signing this summer. But director Matthew Harding says "time has to be right to buy new players. I'm almost sure our new players have almost cost us nothing."

Managing director Colin Hutchinson has admitted Vialli's signing-on fee and £25,000-a-week wages are being paid for out of existing club resources.

Total commitment. Steve Walsh climbing high to win yet another header.

–LEGENDS–

Steve Walsh

Bought for £100,000 by Bryan Hamilton in 1986, Steve Walsh's time with Leicester had the worst possible start with a relegation campaign followed next season by an 11-game ban for a violent clash with David Geddis.

He vowed to learn from that, and did, even though a Football League record of 13 red cards in his career would suggest that the red mist might have descended at any given moment.

Walsh brought honest commitment, total endeavour, and fabulous loyalty to the cause for a succession of managers throughout his 14 seasons with the club.

Made captain by Brian Little, he spent most of his career at the club as a powerful defender, whose feuds with Steve Bull were the brutal stuff of legend.

But he had another string to his bow, used at other times as an equally forceful centre-forward with the knack of coming up with big goals at vital times.

His 15 strikes in the 1992–93 season were pivotal to earning a place at Wembley, and even if that day ended in disappointment, it merely fired the ambition for seasons to come.

A year later his two goals against Derby at Wembley earned a place in the Premier League – and he had the honour of being captain of the side which beat Crystal Palace in 1996 to regain top-flight status.

He remained the heartbeat of the dressing room throughout the Martin O'Neill era, setting up goals in both the Wembley draw with Middlesbrough and the League Cup final replay victory which followed.

FOOTBALL –STATS–

Steve Walsh

Name: Steven Walsh
Born: November 1964
Playing career: 1982–2002
Clubs: Wigan, Leicester City, Norwich, Coventry
Leicester appearances: 449
Goals: 62

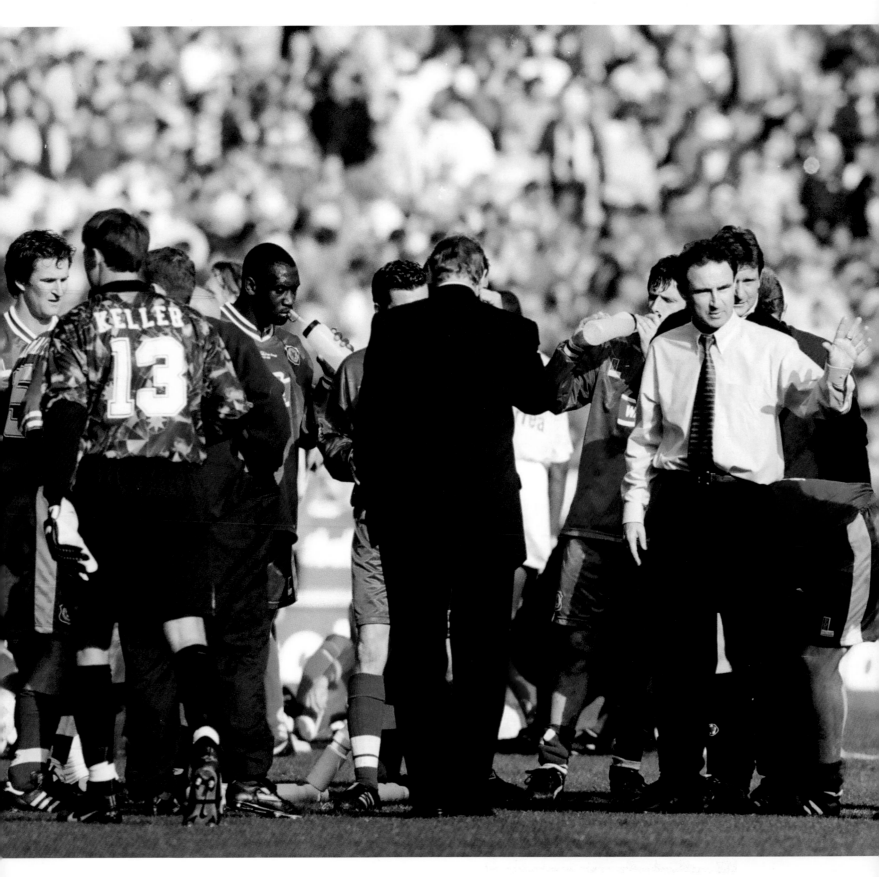

Wembley is a Second Home

Martin O'Neill had found a settled side he could trust in winning promotion, and they settled easily to the Premier League finishing in the top 10.

Barely 10 months after the play-off final City were back at Wembley, this time in the final of the League Cup after edging out Wimbledon on away goals.

There was more drama to come. With seconds ticking on the clock and Middlesbrough, managed by Bryan Robson, in the lead, Emile Heskey came up with an equalizer that would take the tie to a replay.

LEFT: Martin O'Neill hands out advice as Leicester's players prepare for extra-time.

BELOW: Flamboyant Italian Fabrizio Ravanelli puts Boro in front.

COCA-COLA FINAL CRUNCH ★ COCA-COLA FINAL CRUNCH ✦ COCA-COLA FINAL CRUNCH

I've been told to destroy Juno
IT'S IMMORAL

By DAVID MOORE

GENIUS: Juninho will kill teams stone-dead if he's not stopped

SOCCER genius Juninho was last night told: "I have been asked to destroy you and it is immoral!"

Leicester star Pontus Kaamark has sparked a massive row on the eve of the Coca-Cola Cup Final replay.

Swedish international Kaamark is expected to shadow every step taken by Juninho, Middlesbrough's brilliant little Brazilian, tonight.

Kaamark, booked when he did exactly the same job at Wembley, revealed last night: "I apologised to Juninho at the end of the first game.

"Football is supposed to be an entertainment. It is a part of show business these days.

Field

"That means the public are always hoping to see world-class stars like Juninho allowed to express themselves on the field of play.

"I am good at the man-marking role and if the manager asks me to do it again I will follow his wishes.

"But it makes me a destroyer of the public's pleasure — and I do not regard that task as a moral act."

Conscience-stricken Kaamark, who cost £600,000 from Gothenburg, confessed: "I cannot really enjoy such a role.

"The crowd will want to watch Juninho's skills,

SAYS LEICESTER HATCHET MAN

PONTUS KAAMARK

yet it is necessary for me to prevent him from performing.

"Of course, no team enjoys it very much when a highly-talented opponent such as Juninho makes them look foolish.

"So I must try to stop him, because above everything else is the need to help Leicester win the cup and qualify for Europe."

Controversial Kaamark was in trouble recently after reports that he had accused British players of drinking too much beer instead of training hard.

Drink

Now his latest blast could offend the competition's sponsors, plus City's own big-money backers Walkers Crisps.

He said: "Back home in Sweden, footballers are not allowed to drink Coca-Cola or similar products.

"And potato crisps are also banned, because the fat and carbohydrates they contain are considered unhealthy." Leicester boss Martin O'Neill snapped: "Kaamark can continue any moral debate once he discovers whether he is actually on the team bus travelling to Hillsborough.

"Nobody loves the sight of Juninho in full flow more than me, except when he is doing it against Leicester City.

Defeat

"Juninho killed us dead inside 45 minutes in the Premiership meeting at Filbert Street recently.

"I can't afford to risk that happening again.

"If you offer me the pick of victory in a game which stinks the place out or glorious defeat, then I'm bound to choose the win.

"At this stage of Leicester's development, less than a year since we gained promotion, lifting one of the major trophies and the UEFA Cup place which accompanies it would be absolutely wonderful for the club."

PASSION-KILLER: Pontus Kaamark tackles Juninho at Wembley

GAZZA'S OK

PAUL GASCOIGNE returned to action last night as Rangers won 6-0 as managerless Raith Rovers and relegated them.

Gascoigne, who had been out since January 25 with ankle damage, came on after 70 minutes for Brian Laudrup.

Gordan Petric, Gordon Durie (two), David Robertson, Laudrup and Ally McCoist scored to put Rangers 12 points clear of Celtic with a goal difference better by 17.

They cannot now be overtaken on points. Celtic have to win their remaining four matches and Rangers lose three if the Ibrox men are to be deprived of a ninth successive title.

RUDDOCK: Talks

RUDDOCK: I'M OFF

By RICHARD TANNER

ANGRY Neil Ruddock last night rocked Liverpool by admitting: "I've got no future here."

And he is prepared to sacrifice a £2million fortune by quitting Anfield this summer.

Ruddock signed a four-year contract worth £10,000-a-week earlier this season but says: "There's no point me staying here if I'm not in the team. I signed a great contract and I could earn a fortune by just sitting on it, but I'm not like that. I want first team football."

West Ham are prepared to bring the former Spurs star back to London – and Liverpool will sell if the Hammers, or anybody, offer around £3m. Frustrated Ruddock, 28, has started only one game in three months, and the final straw came on Sunday when he was axed from the subs bench.

That snub came five days after Ruddock opted out of a reserve game designed to give him match practice. Now he is demanding showdown talks with boss Roy Evans to sort out his future.

Middlesbrough had the flair of Italian Fabrizio Ravanelli and the intricate ball skills of Brazilian Juninho – Leicester had unquenchable belief and team spirit.

Swedish international Pontus Kåmark might have had doubts about the job he was asked to do both at Wembley and Hillsborough, but he carried out his orders to the letter.

With no goals in 90 minutes it meant the anxiety of extra-time, and then, yet again, Steve Claridge came up with a big goal in a big game.

Leicester's Pontus Kåmark reveals
the battle plan.

Steve Claridge whirls away to
celebrate the winner.

–LEGENDS–

Steve Claridge

On statistics alone, Steve Claridge wouldn't get near the status of Leicester legend. He netted just 20 goals in all from 79 games. But if ever there was a man who delivered quality rather than quantity it was Claridge, the socks-down, scruffy soul who looked every inch the non-League player until he was offered a sight of goal when he suddenly became Premier League class.

He brought with him a sense of fun and adventure, meaning his influence in the dressing room was one of the sparks that set the Martin O'Neill era alight after inauspicious beginnings. He paid back every penny of his £1.2 million transfer fee from Birmingham with interest, many times over.

As if his moment of glory scoring the last-minute goal which won the play-off final in O'Neill's first season wasn't enough, he then wrote his name in lights a second time with the winner that delivered Leicester's first major trophy in 33 years.

As a character he was loved and as a footballer he was far more than just a clinical finisher – a willing worker with his back to goal who chased every lost cause and could pick out a pass to find a team-mate when required.

FOOTBALL —STATS—

Steve Claridge

Name: Stephen Edward Claridge

Born: April 1966

Playing career: 1983–2012

Main clubs: Bournemouth, Weymouth, Aldershot, Cambridge, Luton, Birmingham, Leicester City, Portsmouth, Millwall, Wycombe, Bradford

Leicester appearances: 79

Goals: 20

MIRROR SPORT ++ BEST FOR LATE NIGHT SOCCER ACTION

Leicester 1 Middlesbro 0

LOVE AND CLARIDGE!

GLORY BOYS: Martin O'Neill and goal hero Steve Claridge celebrate Pics: ALBERT COOPER

By JOHN EDWARDS

STEVE CLARIDGE put Leicester into Europe and Martin O'Neill into dreamland at Hillsborough last night.

The ragamuffin frontrunner plays with his socks rolled down to his ankles from first whistle to last.

But they don't come any smarter when it's a matter of snapping up priceless goals.

Claridge drilled a last-gasp winner into the top corner of Crystal Palace's net to book Leicester's Premiership place in the play-offs final last May.

And he was the man of the moment again as he sent Leicester staggering over the finishing line in this Coca-Cola Cup final marathon.

Weary

Claridge suddenly wasn't the only one with his socks down as the tie again went into extra time.

Two sets of players had to drag weary limbs through thirty more gruelling minutes.

But Claridge despatched thoughts of a penalty shoot-out with one swing of his right boot.

Skipper Steve Walsh rose at the far post to meet Garry Parker's deep, 100th-minute free-kick with a towering header back across the box.

It fell perfectly for Claridge, who swung round on instinct to volley a close-range chance beyond Ben Roberts in the Middlesborough goal.

"I can't believe what has happened," said Claridge. "It's beyond my wildest dreams.

"Everybody was knackered, so we thought that one goal would win it.

"I'm so pleased for the whole club and the rest of the lads, who battled their hearts out.

"People have been writing us off since we arrived in the Premiership at the start of the season. This is one hell of a way to prove them wrong."

O'Neill had seen his fighters snatch this replay through teenager Emile Heskey's equaliser with less than three minutes of the original Wembley final left.

O'Neill said: "This won't sink in for a week, it won't sink in for a month.

"My players showed passion and desire, pushed on by our fantastic supporters. I thought we deserved the victory.

"But I must add how very sorry I feel for Bryan Robson and his assistant Viv Anderson because Boro are a decent club and an excellent side."

Jumping

O'Neill was his usual jack-in-the-box self as he stood by the Leicester bench kicking every ball and jumping for every header.

And he still found the energy to race to the touchline when Boro midfielder Emerson fell theatrically to the ground and appealed in vain for a free-kick.

The Leicester boss applauded Martin Bodenham's decision in an act that clearly signalled his feelings about the Brazilian midfielder.

O'Neill's inspirational leadership steered Leicester to a promotion that they have more than consolidated this season.

Now he has landed a bonus that is surely beyond their wildest expectations — a place in the UEFA Cup.

And though Boro had their share of attacking ideas in a replay that put Wembley's dreary deadlock to shame, it was hard to quibble with the outcome.

Leicester went agonisingly close in the 39th minute when Heskey fastened on to a Neil Lennon pass and shot past Roberts.

The big striker was on the point of saluting his second goal of the final when the ball bounced back off the inside of the far post.

Boro brought the best out of Kasey Keller through Craig Hignett in the ninth minute and Juninho in the 34th.

The Leicester keeper was up to it each time with a mixture of reflexes and sure handling.

And he had the Leicester hoards behind his goal chanting "USA" with a brilliant stop within seconds of Claridge's golden goal. Emerson played a one-two with Hignett on the edge of the box and was clean through with just Keller to beat.

But Keller made a crucial block that was just as important as Claridge's 14th strike of the season.

At the end there was simply no consoling Fabrizio Ravanelli and the rest of the Boro players. Particularly Ravanelli.

The Italian international threw his boots to the turf in disgust when Boro let the lead slip through their fingers in extra-time at Wembley.

Misery

Those boots stayed on this time, probably because he couldn't muster the strength to rip them off after another punishing 120 minutes.

Boro's £7million record buy was close to tears as he shrugged aside all attempts to coax him out of his misery.

Finally he accepted a handshake from Heskey, who walked away with Ravanelli's shirt.

Meanwhile skipper Walsh collected the man-of-the-match award as well as the Cup itself.

Party Time

Leicester's players and staff – complete with mascot Filbert Fox – enjoy their big moment at Hillsborough.

–LEGENDS–

Emile Heskey

Leicester's fans already knew about Emile Heskey when Martin O'Neill arrived at the club. A local lad who played for England Schoolboys, he had been thrust into a side hit by injury and illness to make his debut the previous March aged 17.

O'Neill took one look at the raw pace and power of the teenager and threw him straight into his starting team.

For the next four seasons he was one of the first names on the team sheet. Never a prolific scorer of goals, he was an industrious creator of chances for others.

A dozen goals in the 1996–97 season included the all-important equalizer at Wembley that earned a League Cup final replay and ultimately the trophy.

His ability to make those around him look better was not always appreciated by fans, but he was loved by his team-mates.

It also gained him recognition from England manager Kevin Keegan who presented him with the first of 62 caps before he became the club's most expensive outgoing transfer, joining Liverpool in an £11 million deal in 2000.

FOOTBALL –STATS–

Emile Heskey

Name: Emile William Ivanhoe Heskey

Born: January 1978

Playing career: 1994–2012

Main clubs: Leicester City, Liverpool, Birmingham, Wigan, Aston Villa

Leicester appearances: 197

Goals: 46

England appearances: 62

Goals: 7

Emile Heskey's six appearances for different clubs in League Cup finals is a record. He is pictured in action for Leicester against Middlesbrough (main and top right) and Tranmere (bottom right).

By the summer of 1998, O'Neill's success at Leicester had made him a man in demand. First Everton, and then Leeds, attempted to lure him away against a backdrop of behind-the-scenes disputes over funding to further strengthen the team.

In the end, those who had the biggest say were the fans – they mounted an emotional demonstration during a Monday night

PAGE 52　　THE MIRROR, Friday, May 29

O'Neill to go if crisis talks fail

CONCERNED: O'Neill

MARTIN O'NEILL will decide whether to quit Leicester City after showdown talks with the club's new hierarchy.

He flies back to Britain this weekend, after a club tour of Florida, for a top-level meeting to discuss his "serious concerns" about sweeping boardroom changes.

The board has been abolished and a new five-man football committee, including O'Neill, is now in charge.

But O'Neill, who only discovered about the new set-up on Teletext, has threatened to quit unless changes are made.

The Irishman has already clashed with chief executive Barrie Pierpoint and has made it clear he will stay only on his terms.

A Filbert Street source said: "He wants to honour his contract, but if the talks are not in his favour over the next few days there is no doubt he will want to leave."

Leicester's fans are launching a campaign to keep O'Neill at Filbert Street by flooding the club with forms declaring: "I back Martin".

O'Neill quit Norwich City after a similar bust-up with the then chairman Robert Chase two-and-a-half years ago.

And the fans are painfully aware that manageress Celtic and Sheffield Wednesday are keeping tabs on his position, along with Everton.

ROY Keane is cancelling a sunshine holiday to prepare for next season.

The Manchester United skipper is working flat out to reach peak fitness for the start of pre-season friendlies at the end of July.

Keane, out of action for eight months after suffering cruciate ligament damage, checks in at United's training ground each morning. And after shedding a stone in weight, he's looking to jet out with United for their Scandinavian tour.

O'NEILL'S THREAT TO QUIT

Turmoil club worries boss

By DAVID MOORE

UNHAPPY: Martin O'Neill wants to know what is happening at Leicester

MARTIN O'NEILL will consider quitting as Leicester's boss unless the troubled Midland club come up with the answers he is demanding.

Coca-Cola Cup winner O'Neill, rated one of the best managers in British football, believes Leicester are in danger of heading in the wrong direction.

Further in-fighting this week, which saw Tom Smeaton kicked out as chairman and also removed from the plc board, has cast a further cloud over Filbert Street.

It threatens to wreck O'Neill's ambitious plans to the down future such as Emile Heskey, Neil Lennon and Matt Elliott as money deals to prevent them being lured away.

O'Neill, 45, is already on the short list to take over at new Scottish champions Celtic, and is also being linked with the Everton job if Howard Kendall goes.

A source close to O'Neill confirmed last night: "Martin is desperately unhappy at the turn of events, because he feels Leicester may not give him sufficient backing.

Stadium

"Coupled with the delay in identifying a site for the proposed new stadium, it all adds up to a considerable question mark in Martin's mind about what the future holds."

O'Neill is due to take Leicester's players on a ten-day trip to Florida next Monday, which will delay any serious negotiations over what happens next at Leicester.

England Under-21 striker Heskey, Northern Ireland midfielder Lennon and Kasey Keller, America's World Cup keeper, all have only one season remaining on their current deals.

O'Neill insists: "We have to sort out the business of improving Leicester's restrictive wage scale as a matter of priority. It really can't wait."

Long-serving skipper Steve Walsh warned recently: "Unless pay packets are boosted considerably, Leicester's best players will go elsewhere — and you can bet that Martin will follow."

O'Neill's own contract includes a get-out clause, allowing any interested club to buy up the remaining two years for an estimated £750,000.

But such is O'Neill's reputation following 30 months of success at Leicester, where Wembley triumph and a taste of European competition quickly followed promotion, there would be no shortage of bidders.

While O'Neill is carefully refusing to comment at the moment, he admitted last week: "You can never never shout anything to do with soccer these days. Everything changes.

"While I would still expect to be in charge at Leicester when the season kicks off in August, it is sometimes difficult to see that far ahead. I enjoy myself here, and I want to continue enjoying life as a manager."

Dublin showdown

By DAVID MOORE

DION DUBLIN faces make-or-break talks with Coventry over a new contract.

With only one year left on his current deal, 23-goal Dublin has stalled so far on Coventry's offer of £16,000 a week.

But now chairman Bryan Richardson plans fresh talks with skipper Dublin, named in England's 30-strong provisional World Cup party.

It could lead to a compromise being thrashed out with the Sky Blues tabling increased wages of £18,000 a week to persuade Dublin to sign a three-year agreement.

Richardson said: "We are determined to make sure Dion stays at Highfield Road."

Dublin's agent, Jon Holmes, said: "The ball is in Coventry's court. We need the right package.

"The alternative is clear – Dion will simply sit tight during next season, then exercise his freedom of contract and walk away with a free transfer which leaves the club empty-handed."

IZZET ENOUGH TO

Muzzy
messag
for Mar

John DILLON

Leicester 2 Spurs 1

GEORGE GRAHAM be a happy man Tottenham's fans c hold him as dearly Leicester's fans wors Martin O'Neill.

A defeat in his opening g was not exactly the greates chat-up lines, even if it inflicted by two goals spectacular quality.

But it was an extraordi night of emotion at Fil Street, when Leicester's showed that maybe troubled old game has a bi somewhere after all.

Quite simply, Graham's de in the Tottenham dug-out overshadowed by the drama impassioned pleading of 2 fans for O'Neill to resist the of Leeds and stay put on own bench.

And after a truly touch experience like that, possible even to believe that one-time King of Highbury eventually be loved by all White Hart Lane.

Concerned

Not that he's yet intereste that. George will surely morning be concerned o that his new charg committed what he regard a cardinal sin and chuc away an early lead.

The new era dawned o briefly for Spurs after Ferdinand gave them a surp 12th-minute lead.

Then it was a slow but s return to more uncertain tin as Leicester, driven by drama of the occasion and feeling of the crowd, turne all around.

If O'Neill is about to walk and head up the M1 — and way he talked last night seems likely — Emile Hes and Muzzy Izzet delivered go which made it a fitting fina

Heskey's sheer physical po

CITY

FROM BACK PAGE

a lot of work to be don Second half substitute Pa Armstrong missed a sup chance to put Spurs in fr late in the game.

And hapless Swiss defen Ramon Vega was criticised Graham after he had earl allowed Heskey to escape score Leicester's equaliser.

"It looked as if it would 1-1 and if Armstrong had sco we'd have won," added Grah

O'NEILL WILL GET £15m KITTY

By IAN EDWARDS

O'NEILL: Tempting offer

LEEDS UNITED are ready to hand Martin O'Neill a transfer kitty of £15million to persuade him to leave Leicester City.

United are determined to quash rumours that George Graham quit Elland Road because of a lack of spending power.

Leeds have already said they will make O'Neill one of the biggest earners in the Premiership with a £750,000-a-year contract for the next three seasons.

And they are ready to provide the cash needed to help him assemble a team capable of challenging for the Premiership title.

O'Neill, 46, has operated on a strict budget at Leicester, who know the lure of large finance could be decisive in the battle for the highly-rated Ulsterman.

Leeds chairman Peter Ridsdale said: "We are one of the biggest clubs in the country. We expect success and we know that takes financing.

"Over the last two seasons we have been one of the biggest net spenders in the Premiership and that shows our ambition. We were prepared to back that up again with George Graham.

"I resent suggestions that we were not prepared to give him money to sign players."

Leicester plc chairman Sir Rodney Walker has admitted that if O'Neill wishes to talk to Leeds, there is little he can do to prevent him. Ridsdale is urging him to face the situation head on.

Ridsdale said: "I want Leicester to ask Martin O'Neill outright if he wishes to talk to us and to see what he says. As far as I'm concerned, the ball is in Martin's court.

"If he says he has no interest in coming to Leeds, we will have to re-think.

"To the best of my knowledge, he has not said that. So he remains our only target."

Coventry have already warned Leeds off Gordon Strachan. If O'Neill snubs them, they are likely to hand the job to David O'Leary and assistant Eddie Gray, at least until the end of the season.

CITY GENTS: Robbie Savage celebrates with scorer Muzzy Izzet after (inset left) Les Ferdinand put Spurs ahead only for Emile Heskey to level

win over Tottenham that made their manager feel wanted by the supporters.

It appeared there might be an uneasy truce with chairman John Elsom, but once O'Neill had given his word to stay, he threw heart and soul into taking the team forward.

IN A RAGE: Boss George Graham barks out orders as his Spurs flops crash

Martin mania floors George

By JOHN DILLON

Leicester 2 Spurs 1

GEORGE GRAHAM'S first match in charge of Tottenham was over-shadowed by emotional Leicester protests to keep Martin O'Neill.

But now City boss O'Neill is poised to break Leicester's hearts by walking out to join Leeds.

A blizzard of banners proclaiming: 'Don't Go Martin' were raised during the 2-1 defeat of Spurs, which wrecked Graham's first big night in charge.

O'Neill was given a standing ovation before and after the match. But his comments afterwards suggested he is ready to move to Elland Road.

Promise

He said: "I will make my decision in the next 24 hours. I promise you that. But I'm a goodly way towards making my mind up.

"I accept I'll not be allowed to talk to Leeds while I am still in the job here."

Meanwhile, Graham confessed he has a big job on his hands after Spurs chucked away an early advantage.

Les Ferdinand gave Tottenham a 12th minute lead but spectacular goals from Emile Heskey and Muzzy Izzet claimed victory for Leicester.

Graham said: "I wouldn't criticise my team's commitment, but there is

TURN TO PAGE 51

MAKE YOU STAY?

CAN'T BEAR IT: The campaign to keep Martin O'Neill at Filbert Street is never far away from the Leicester manager as supporters make their protest

**duced the first in the 36th minute and a stunning, opportunist volley from Izzet handed victory to O'Neill and **ening night defeat to Graham **he 84th minute.

housands of specially-inted banners were raised as Neill, decked out in his **miliar sloppy sweatshirt, **erged from the tunnel.

**e message was simple, but **artfelt and deeply sincere: **on't go, Martin."

**ottenham's fans were the **st to get something to shout **out after 12 minutes, when **rdinand decided to make a **ick impression on new boss **aham by firing Spurs ahead.

**uel Fox threaded a pass **ong the right flank. Then **rren Anderson scooped in a **pically tricky, curling cross **d Ferdinand escaped his **arker and slid in to touch **me his third strike of the **ason from a few yards out.

**Anderson was in the role he

MATCH STATS		
LEICESTER v TOTTENHAM		
	GOALS	
2		1
7	SHOTS ON TARGET	6
9	SHOTS OFF TARGET	5
1	BLOCKED SHOTS	2
7	CORNERS	2
0	FOULS CONCEDED	15
1	OFFSIDES	3
	RED CARD	0
	YELLOW CARDS	1

likes best, bounding around in central midfield while David Ginola and Stephen Clemence eagerly switched flanks in search of openings.

They were still pretty scarce, though, and Ginola was way off target when he aimed a 25-yard shot high in the 18th minute.

The muscular Heskey became an increasingly potent threat as the first-half wore on and Sol Campbell was eventually booked for pulling him down in the 31st minute.

The England defender had

already made a desperate clearance when Steve Guppy's left-wing corner floated in dangerously.

And Heskey was finally rewarded for his strenuous persistence.

The burly Heskey against the ponderous Swiss Ramon Vega? No contest!

And after the inevitable escape into freedom in the box, Heskey scored with a glorious, powerful rising drive from 12 yards.

Touchline

But Tottenham hadn't posed any threat in the second-half and Ginola was called off and replaced by Chris Armstrong in the 66th minute.

Ginola will certainly not have impressed Graham by collecting a 58th-minute yellow card for back-chatting a linesman.

But Armstrong then promptly fluffed Tottenham's best chance of the second half when Anderton sent him charging forward with three yards on his nearest challenger.

His shot went straight at

Spurs got an unwelcome chance to show their new chief whether they have the quality he admires so intensely — defensive resolve. At least Anderton most surely displayed it when he raced deep into his own half in the 64th minute to tackle Heskey.

After that it was Vega who had to be firm to scoop the ball off the feet of Cottee as he darted hungrily around the edge of the six-yard box.

keeper Kasey Keller. There was a minor fright for Leicester when Campbell scooped a half-hearted lob into the box and keeper Kelley misjudged it, only to claim it safely at the second attempt.

But then Izzet gave the evening the finish it really deserved in glorious fashion.

After Ferdinand cleared Guppy's free-kick, the ball spun invitingly into the air around 25 yards out but directly in Izzet's line of fire.

He answered the challenge with a brilliantly struck volley which perhaps deserved a standing ovation of its own.

That, though, was reserved for O'Neill again at the end. The question now is whether he listens to his heart or his head.

LEICESTER: Keller, Savage, Guppy, Sinclair, Elliott, Taggart (Campbell 46, Parker 87), Izzet, Lennon, Ullathorne, Heskey, Cottee.

TOTTENHAM: Baardsen, Carr, Calderwood, Fox, Anderton, Ferdinand, Edinburgh, Ginola (Armstrong 66), Vega, Campbell, Clemence (Dominguez 87).

LOSING O'NEILL BATTLE

**Heskey rolled Vega too easily r their first goal.

Leicester last night accused eds — who named a new boss cause Graham quit to join purs — of making illegal tempts to lure O'Neill to orkshire.

Asked if he may have to quit n order to talk to Leeds, Neill replied: "That's the enario as I understand it.

He then added ironically: "The owd reaction was certainly fferent to the 30th March, 1996

when we lost at home to Sheffield United. It was very emotional tonight, though.

"In the last couple of years they've been fantastic and trying to make a balanced judgment this evening is difficult.

"We were all over the shop in the first 15 minutes but we pulled it round. It was a great equalising goal and a great winning goal."

Leicester chairman John Elsom said: "The Leeds chairman can say what he likes but it seems to me he's breaking the

great manager and we'd like him to stay.

"We've offered Martin an improved deal and an extended contract and we continue to talk things through. I want him to want to stay."

Leicester were infuriated by the comments of Leeds chief Peter Ridsdale, who said at the weekend he wants O'Neill to give him a call.

Izzet led a players' plea for O'Neill to remain at Filbert Street, saying: "He's been a

code of conduct of the Premier League chairmen.

Graham added: "This is the way football is going. It is no surprise managers are being transferred. Certain managers are being head-hunted.

"Leeds put a price on my head. If they hadn't I'd still be there."

ELSOM: ...st-d Leeds

David MOORE

MARTIN O'NEILL turned his back on Leeds yesterday by agreeing to stay at Leicester.

But even if O'Neill signs a new four-year contract chairman John Elsom might find himself waving that scrap of paper in the air, claiming: "Peace in our time", only to discover that a fresh war has broken out over his manager's future.

Elsom sat at O'Neill's right shoulder to hear the 46-year-old boss declare: "I am staying. But for how long, well, an answer to that particular question is totally imponderable."

"Leicester won't let me talk to Leeds about the possibility of succeeding George Graham as their boss, despite a gentleman's agreement to the contrary.

"I can only think that Mr Elsom is suffering from Alzheimer's disease. How else do you explain how he forgets so easily what was said between us during the summer?

"Let me put it this way, while I have no desire to fall out with John, I don't suppose I will continue to enjoy going out for dinner with him.

"Although I'm no saint, nor does this matter centre around money, I simply feel that I have been denied my rights."

O'Neill led Leicester to promotion before lifting the Coca-Cola Cup to gain their first European passport in 38 years. Privately, he admits to growing reservations about whether he can carry the modest Midland outfit much further towards the soccer summit.

O'Neill, whose basic salary before bonuses will be bumped up to $500,000, admitted: "It would be ridiculous of me not to agree on the dotted line. It's interesting, isn't it, that an improved contract should suddenly materialise almost out of thin air.

"One of those remarkable coincidences. Who knows when, or even whether, another club of comparable size will ever want me again?

"I shall not forget recent events in a hurry. My personal ambition has always been to win the European Cup, like

PLEA: Fans urge O'Neill to stay

Brian Clough did twice when I played for Nottingham Forest.

"These days, there are only five or six clubs who can hold genuine aspirations attacking that target. Historically, Leeds United number among them. The Leeds affair is over. But I will not make the same mistake twice, so any Leicester contract will contain 194 special clauses all written

DON'T GO: O'Neill discovers the warmth of Leicester fans' appreciation as he is stopped outside Filbert Street yesterday

HAPPY TO STAY? YOU'RE JOKING!

O'Neill: I'm here for now, but don't hold your breath

Saint

"The chairman has referred to what he sees as my honesty and integrity, yet can't trust himself to let me speak with Leeds," added O'Neill.

"I would have entered any such talks with a completely open mind. I should not need to remind Mr Elsom that I turned down both Nottingham Forest and Leicester when I was manager of Wycombe.

in block capitals."

O'Neill pledged: "In the meantime, I shall work my hardest to help Leicester with football matches. I don't know any other way.

"The support I have received from Leicester's players and fans alike helped me sort out my mind. I simply couldn't walk away.

"I want several other players like Muzzy Izzet and Matt Elliott to follow Emile Heskey and Neil Lennon by accepting new contracts. We must also aim to attract good players here to build our strength.

"Provided I can get on with the job free from interference, all Mr Elsom will hear from me in the usual fortnightly question about how much we have to spend.

But O'Neill warned: "I have kept my part of the bargain and after the Leeds disap-

FAILED FIGHT TO LAND O'NEILL

OCT 1: Leeds lose boss George Graham to Spurs. Gordon Strachan and Martin O'Neill head their shortlist. Leicester warn Leeds not to approach O'Neill.

OCT 2: David O'Leary says he does not wish to replace Graham permanently.

OCT 4: O'Neill swears he has had no approach from Leeds.

OCT 10-11: Leeds chairman Peter Ridsdale makes unsuccessful attempts to gain permission to talk to O'Neill.

OCT 15: O'Neill he wants to speak to Leeds to hear what they have to say.

OCT 16: Leeds call off hunt for O'Neill and put O'Leary in charge for trip to Forest. But speculation remains that O'Neill is still the wanted man.

OCT 19: Ridsdale says October 21 is deadline for O'Neill.

OCT 21: Leicester confirm O'Neill is staying – and Leeds appoint O'Leary.

pointment, the board had better keep theirs.

"When I say 'no interference' I mean no interference'. The club's chief executive, Barrie Pierpoint, reckons there is no friction between us. The man must be hallucinating."

His voice laced with scorn, O'Neill explained: "My job is to produce a successful side. Barrie Pierpoint's job is to build a new stadium for Leicester. It has already been

delayed for 12 months. My 14-year-old daughter could do it, and she'd do it more quickly!"

Leeds will today appoint David O'Leary as manager. He will sign a £1.5m three-year deal and be handed a £12m transfer kitty.

Elsom, clearly in a quandary over whether to laugh or cry, confessed: "I had not understood the intensity of Martin's feelings."

Back to (Wembley) Business as Usual

Almost immediately Leicester's fortunes got back on track, with a run of late results producing a third successive top-10 finish in the Premier League – and yet another trip to a League Cup final.

This one ended in disappointment, however, as for once Leicester were on the wrong end of a late Wembley goal when Allan Nielsen scored for 10-man Spurs.

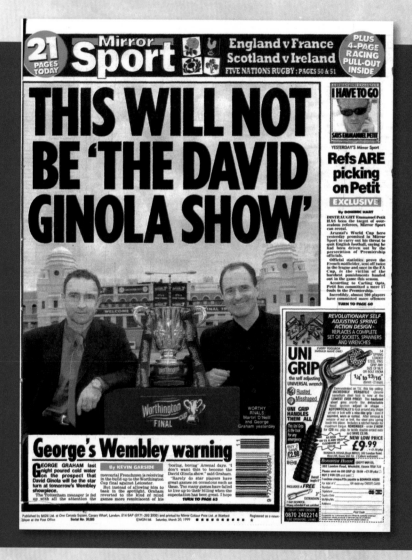

WORTHINGTON CUP FINAL — LEICESTER v TOTTENHAM

GEORGE · THE THIRST

e moment for Spurs as

Graham launches new glory era

Harry HARRIS

Leicester 0 Tottenham 1

GEORGE Graham's transformation of a motley crew of no-hopers into cup winners is just the start of what promises to be a new odyssey of success in North London.

This competition was the launch pad of Graham's glittering run of success that ended with a massive collection of silverware at Highbury.

And maybe he is beginning it all over again with their fiercest rivals.

The league cup has been a particular favourite of Graham's and his third triumph launches him into joint second place with Bob Paisley in the all-time list of managerial success behind Brian Clough, who won this tournament four times.

Even with 10 men for the second part of the second half Spurs were too good for a brave but limited Leicester team under the guidance of Martin O'Neill.

Graham drank champagne out of a plastic mug in the Wembley dressing-room, where his chairman Alan Sugar was drenched when he joined the celebrations.

Sugar must take the credit for having the guts to appoint the manager previously in charge of Arsenal.

Hostile

The fact that Graham came from Elland Road made little difference. He was steeped in the Highbury traditions, but Sugar was convinced he would turn around those hostile feelings.

Indeed, Graham has turned out to be the messiah rather than the devil from the hated rival camp and there was an almighty cheer when Graham lifted the Worthington Cup.

Graham performed his trade-mark trick of celebrating a goal that never was when Steffen Iversen scraped the outside of a post and hit the side-netting.

Graham leapt up punching the air in delight, shouting: "Yes!" — only for the realisation to sink in that it wasn't a goal.

It was the closest Spurs had come, nearly ten minutes after going down to ten men when left back Justin Edinburgh was shown the red card, while Robbie Savage was only booked by referee Terry Heilbron.

Savage barged into Edinburgh, the only surviving member of Spurs' last success of any description, when they won the FA Cup eight years ago.

Edinburgh reacted by lashing out his hand at Savage, landing it on his head. While not an outright punch, that kind of retaliation was highly risky and he paid the ultimate price.

The match degenerated into a free-for-all in the 84th minute when Savage challenged Graham's German midfield signing Steffen Freund.

Savage was furious that Freund over-elaborated his dive and feigned injury in a seemingly deliberate attempt to even up the score — a second yellow card would have sent Savage back to the dressing-room.

When the crowd of 77,892 were informed of the three minutes of injury time at the end of a sub-standard final, O'Neill decided to take off Savage before he was sent off.

The final seemed to be heading for extra time that would have favoured Leicester when Iversen broke on the right flank.

Predicted

He tore into the penalty area, his shot was scooped upwards by keeper Kasey Keller — and Allan Nielsen launched himself into a diving header for the winner and his nomination for man of the match.

Sol Campbell went up to lift the cup — just as the Spurs fans predicted all along — and his performance will have impressed watching England coach Kevin Keegan.

Spurs have been given a fast track into Europe and Graham has the platform on which to build a new dynasty at White Hart Lane — even if the direction seems to be pure Highbury.

Graham inherited a team of under-achievers from Christian Gross and knocked them into shape far quicker than anyone expected, even the Spurs chairman.

With an FA Cup semi-final to contest against Newcastle, Spurs are confident they will be back at Wembley to compete for a Cup double. Only Graham has previously achieved that, when Arsenal twice beat Sheffield Wednesday in 1993.

He can expect new investment for next season's European campaign and a shot at contesting the bigger prizes with Arsenal, Manchester United and Chelsea.

Wembley was supposed to be the domain of David Ginola.

Spurs had never beaten Leicester since the Foxes entered the Premiership and even lost to their bogey team in Graham's first match in charge with a late Muzzy Izzet screamer at Filbert Street.

With so much attention focused on Ginola and little else developing, it was relatively simply for O'Neill's team to contain the favourites.

In fact it was five minutes from the interval before Spurs managed their first effort on target, a Darren Anderton free kick providing Iversen with a near-post header. But the keeper was well positioned.

But O'Neill had plotted the subduing of the brilliant Juninho two years ago in the Coca-Cola Cup final, where Pontus Kaamark was appointed the Brazilian's shadow.

On this occasion O'Neill instructed Rob Ullathorne to stick with the Frenchman come what may.

Ginola started brightly enough, but Leicester made the first chance in the 21st minute when Tony Cottee fed Savage, whose through-ball eluded Campbell. It gave Emile Heskey sight of goal, but Ramon Vega made a vital tackle.

Yes, the same Vega the Spurs fans used to boo for his incompetence in defence is one of those players Graham has convinced he can perform to his international potential on the Premiership stage.

Cautioned

Matt Elliott was the first to be cautioned for an over-the-top tackle on Vega just before half-time. It threatened to get out of hand after the Edinburgh dismissal, but both teams regained their discipline.

It was never going to be a classic but, once O'Neill got his tactics right to cater for Ginola, neither was it the mis-match some had assumed it was going to be.

Graham has made the first moves towards shifting the balance of power in the capital every so slightly back towards White Hart Lane.

It's just a start, but after so many barren years there was every reason for the knees-up on the pitch.

JUSTIN EDINBURGH MY SHAME: Page 37

WINNING WAYS: Nielsen is first to react after Leicester goalkeeper Kasey Keller can only parry Steffen Iversen's cross

GEORGE GRAHAM'S ROLL OF HONOUR

AS A MANAGER

ARSENAL
- 1987: League Cup
- 1989: Division I championship
- 1991: Division I championship
- 1993: FA Cup, League Cup
- 1994: European Cup Winners' Cup

TOTTENHAM
- 1999: Worthington Cup

MILLWALL
- 1985: Promotion from Division 3

AS A PLAYER
- 1965: League Cup winner after Chelsea beat Leicester
- 1970: Fairs Cup winner
- 1971: Wins the double with the league championship and FA Cup

Final roll call
League championships: 3; FA Cups: 2; League Cups: 4; Fairs Cup: 1; European Cup Winners' Cup: 1; Scotland caps: 12

NIELSEN'S A LAST-GASP HERO

FROM BACK PAGE

Twin Towers appearance when they face Newcastle in the FA Cup semi-finals.

Graham said: "We will enjoy this success, then get on with the job. Winning is the only thing that matters to me.

"That's the direction I intend to travel, and my message to the current squad is simply this — if you want to join me on the trip, then that's great. But it's up to you." Nielsen, 28, playing only because new signing Tim Sherwood was ineligible for yesterday's final, said: "That was definitely the most important goal of my entire career. It is the best feeling I've ever had in my life."

But Tony Cottee's tears summed up Leicester's bitter disappointment at losing in the dying seconds.

Veteran striker Cottee broke down and wept as he watched the Spurs players climb the Wembley steps. Cottee, consoled by City boss Martin O'Neill at the end (right), admitted: "Yes, I was crying — and I was entitled to do so. I have now lost four finals at Wembley, which is pretty hard to bear.

"And when you are my age, 33, you have to wonder whether the opportunity will ever come round again. No wonder they call it the crying game."

TONY Cottee's consoled by Martin O'Neill

hold the Worthington Cup aloft   Picture: BRADLEY ORMESHER

And Back
Again for
More

It had taken Leicester 33 years to win a trophy, but just three seasons to perform the feat again as the side went back to Wembley to play the last League Cup final before the old stadium was demolished.

Skipper Matt Elliott's two goals made it another day to remember.

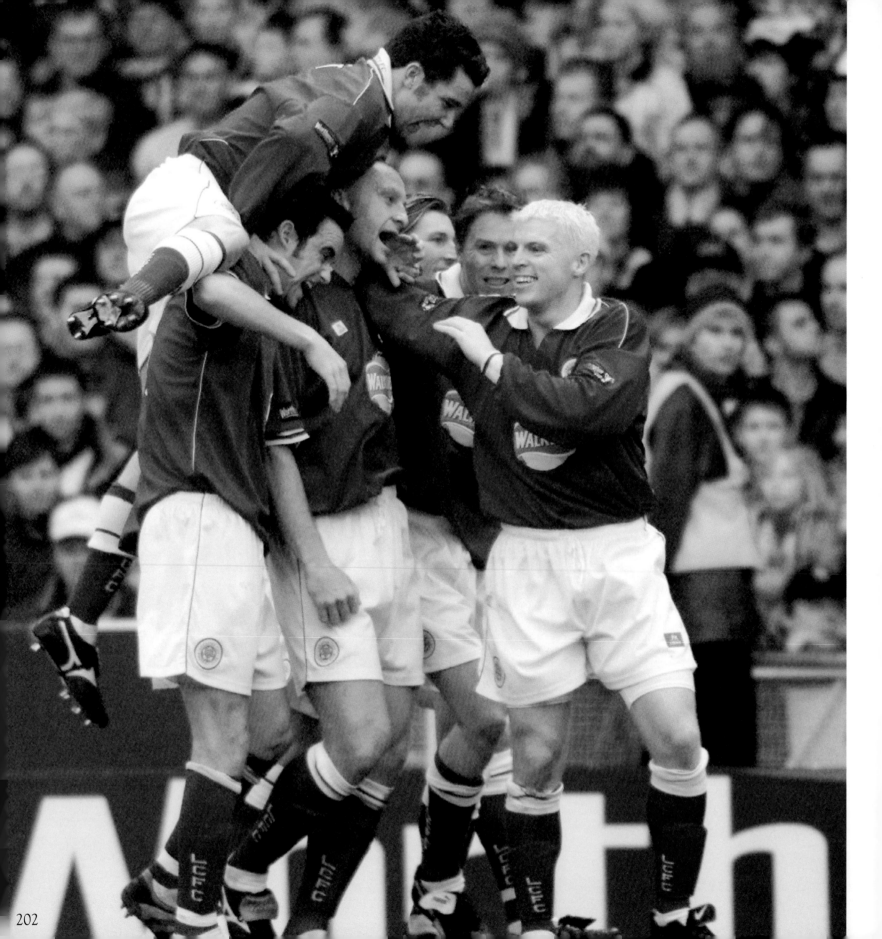

Happy Days

LEFT: Leicester's success was built on team spirit – and the closeness of the players shows.

RIGHT: O'Neill lived and breathed every minute on the touchline – and fans loved sharing the emotion with him.

–LEGENDS–

Matt Elliott

Fans love players who wear their heart on their sleeve and give their all – and nobody better deserved that description than giant centre-half Matt Elliott.

He had been doing exactly that for nearly 10 years around the lower levels of the game when Leicester agreed a club record £1.6 million fee with Oxford to give his skills a new platform in the Premier League.

It was a chance he grabbed eagerly, and within a year of arriving at Filbert Street had stepped up another level to become a Scottish international (thanks to his grandmother's roots north of the border).

His height, heading ability, and rugged skinhead haircut gave him the appearance of being just a ruthless stopper, but when he had the ball at his feet there was far more to his game than that.

To prove it he also filled the role of emergency centre-forward from time to time – and his finest moments came when, as captain, he scored the two goals in the 2000 League Cup final then climbed the Wembley steps to lift the trophy.

FOOTBALL –STATS–

Matt Elliott

Name: Matthew Stephen Elliott

Born: November 1968

Playing career: 1988–2004

Clubs: Charlton, Torquay, Scunthorpe, Oxford, Leicester City

Leicester appearances: 290

Goals: 33

Scotland appearances: 62

Goals: 1

SHEARER: THE VERDICT
PAGES 36 & 37

BABY LOVE

Dad-to-be Elliott is Leicester Cup hero

By JOHN CROSS
Leicester 2 Tranmere 1

LEICESTER hero Matt Elliott will dedicate his Worthington Cup glory to his new baby.

Two-goal Elliott's wife Cathy was at Wembley despite their fourth child being due yesterday. Elliott said: "I've been on tenterhooks for days hoping that she does not go into labour. Now I'm hoping she won't have the baby for another couple of days so I can really go out and celebrate.

"But I'm afraid that maybe the excitement might start things off.

"I kept my eye on her before the match and I kept on looking up during the game and she was jigging about with the best of them."

When asked whether he would now name the new baby Wembley, Elliott joked: "I thought you were supposed to name the baby after where they were conceived, and Back Alley doesn't sound good."

Manager Martin O'Neill is praying that City's ticket to the UEFA Cup will be enough to keep £12m Emile Heskey.

He has only 18 months left on his contract, and O'Neill said:

TURN TO PAGE 39

GOLIATH 2 DAVID 1: Rovers skipper David Kelly is disconsolate after his goal was outdone by the double of giant Leicester captain Matt Elliott

IT'S A JOY: Boss Martin O'Neill congratulates his two-goal skipper and father-to-be Matt Elliott
Pic: BRADLEY ORMESHER

KING CLARKE DESTROYS TIGER

From TONY STENSON

DARREN CLARKE pulled off a remarkable victory over world No.1 Tiger Woods to win the Andersen Consulting Match Play Championship last night. The Ulsterman collected one million dollars after hammering the seemingly unbeatable Woods into submission at the La Costa course in Carlsbad, San Diego.

Clarke's success is the biggest sporting triumph to hit Northern Ireland since Barry McGuigan won the world featherweight boxing title and Mary Peters an Olympic gold medal.

And the 31-year-old Clarke, who won the final 4 & 3 over 36 holes, said: "That has taken some of the intimidation out of playing him. Tiger is unquestionably the number one and the best in the world and we are pretty good friends.

"We were both nip and tuck this morning but I got on a bit of a roll and got my nose in front. But then Tiger being Tiger came back and

TURN TO PAGE 36

Published by MGN Ltd. at One Canada Square, Canary Wharf, London, E14 5AP (0171-293 3000) and printed by Mirror Colour Print Ltd. at Watford
Registered as a newspaper at the Post Office   Serial No. 30,862   ©MGN Ltd.   Monday, February 28, 2000

New Century, New Home
2000-

The new millennium marked a change in football's fortunes as the global commercial power of the Premier League increased the financial stakes at the top of the game.

City's move to a new home in 2002 was designed to cash in on that bonanza, but instead relegation created huge problems from which the club has been recovering since.

Fortunately one thing remains constant, right back to the days when those first players put in ninepence each to buy a ball – the passion of the Leicester public for their football team.

That, more than anything, guarantees more excitement

2000 Peter Taylor takes over. 2001 Taylor sacked and Dave Bassett becomes the new manager with Micky Adams as number two. 2002 Relegation; Adams takes full control; Leicester move to the Walkers Stadium; by October the club is placed in administration with debts of £50 million; Gary Lineker leads a consortium to rescue the club. 2003 Promotion to the Premier League. 2004 Relegation; Adams resigns, Craig Levein takes over. 2006 Levein sacked and David Kelly placed in charge; Milan Mandarić becomes the new owner. 2007 Kelly sacked; Nigel Worthington is manager . . . then he's out and Martin Allen comes in, only to be replaced by Gary Megson. 2008 Megson gone in six weeks, Ian Holloway is next; relegation to third tier; Nigel Pearson the new boss. 2009 Promotion from League One. 2010 Play-off semi-final defeat to Cardiff on a shoot-out; Pearson leaves; Paulo Sousa appointed and dismissed; Sven-Göran Eriksson next in the hot seat after Mandarić sells to new owners King Power. 2011 Pearson returns. 2013 Play-off semi-final defeat.

The Walkers Stadium in this case playing host to
Barwell FC v Loughborough Dynamo in the Westerby Cup final.

When
FOOTBALL Was
FOOTBALL

A big thank you to:

Martin O'Neill, who not only agreed to write the foreword, but cared enough to sit down and do it in his own words with a pen and paper. It's an honour to have this book endorsed by the man who gave Leicester the most successful days of the club's 130 years of history.

Simon Flavin and Vito Inglese for guiding me through the Mirrorpix archives at Watford.
Richard Havers for his help as editor, and everyone at Haynes Publishing for their backing and support.

The generations of *Mirror* reporters, cameramen and production journalists, without whose creative work and professionalism the *Mirror* archives wouldn't have existed in the first place.

Dave Smith and Paul Taylor, who wrote the definitive club history *Of Fossils and Foxes*. Where there have been any inconsistencies in the *Mirror*'s archives, I've used their brilliantly researched work as the defining verdict on appearance figures.

And last in this list, but most important of all, to Sue, Daniel, Matthew, Hayley and Jamie for being the people who inspire me.